Parent Teen
Len McMillan

Also by Len McMillan

The Family of God (And How to Live With Them!)
The Owner's Guide to Male Midlife Crisis
ParentWise (How to Raise Good Adventist Kids)
Person to Person
Slaying Your Dragons
Why Can't My Mate Be More Like Me?

An Adventist counselor
on living with teens—and loving it

REVIEW AND HERALD® PUBLISHING ASSOCIATION
HAGERSTOWN, MD 21740

Copyright © 1993 by
Review and Herald® Publishing Association

The author assumes full responsibility for the accuracy of all facts and quotations as cited in this book.

Texts credited to NIV are from the *Holy Bible, New International Version.* Copyright © 1973, 1978, 1984, International Bible Society. Used by permission of Zondervan Bible Publishers.

Bible texts credited to RSV are from the Revised Standard Version of the Bible, copyright © 1946, 1952, 1971, by the Division of Christian Education of the National Council of the Churches of Christ in the U.S.A. Used by permission.

Verses marked TLB are taken from *The Living Bible,* copyright © by Tyndale House Publishers, Wheaton, Ill. Used by permission.

This book was
Edited by Richard W. Coffen
Designed by Bill Kirstein
Cover design by Helcio Deslandes
Cover photo by Joel D. Springer
Typeset: 12.5/13.5 Sabon

PRINTED IN U.S.A.

98 97 96 95 94 93   10 9 8 7 6 5 4 3 2 1

R & H Cataloging Service
McMillan, Leonard David, 1938–
   Parentteen.

   1. Adolescence. I. Title.
       155.5

ISBN 0-8280-0732-2

Contents

Chapter 1
Uncle Toby 7

Chapter 2
Can This Be My Teen? 19

Chapter 3
Is This Really Me? 35

Chapter 4
Why Can't We Be Friends? 56

Chapter 5
Teaching Your Teens About Relationships 66

Chapter 6
Teaching Your Teens About Sex 82

Chapter 7
Teaching Your Teens About Values 96

Chapter 8
Teaching Your Teens About Love 110

CHAPTER 1

Uncle Toby

Just about the time Elvis Presley made his earthshaking entrance onto the American music scene, Dr. Richard Asher, a London physician, was introduced to Uncle Toby. Dr. Asher had been called to a home to treat a sick child (in those days physicians still made house calls), and he noticed a quiet, immobile man sitting in the corner. Curious, Dr. Asher inquired, "Who's that?"

Without turning to look, one of the family members replied, "That's Uncle Toby—he's hardly moved in seven years."

Strange as it may sound, Uncle Toby had gradually slowed down until he didn't move at all. Family members saw to it that he ate and had water to drink, and someone turned him and occasionally helped him to the toilet. No one in the family seemed to think it strange that Uncle Toby didn't move or speak. He was really no trouble at all. And nobody seemed too concerned about his lack of movement.

Dr. Asher spoke to Uncle Toby, but received no reply. He found a faint pulse and a very cold hand. Somehow it appeared that Uncle Toby was in a state of suspended animation. Because his condition had happened so slowly, the family had grown accustomed to his state and now accepted it as normal for Uncle Toby. However, at the doctor's insistence they allowed Uncle Toby to be taken to the local hospital for testing.

Uncle Toby's body temperature was so low it could not be measured with a regular thermometer. A special thermometer used to measure hypothermia indicated that his temperature was at 68 degrees Fahrenheit, a full 30 degrees below normal. Further testing revealed that Uncle Toby's thyroid had just about shut down completely, and his metabolic rate was almost zero. He was literally in cold storage or suspended animation.

Curing Uncle Toby's problem was fairly simple. All he needed was the thyroid hormone, thyroxine, which released him from his Rip Van Winkle existence. However, the medication had to be administered gradually so that Uncle Toby's organs would be awakened slowly lest he go into cardiac arrest.

Curing Uncle Toby's problem was fairly simple.

After a week of treatment his temperature increased to 72 degrees. Three weeks later it registered 80 degrees, and Uncle Toby began to move and talk, albeit very slowly. He sounded like a phonograph record being played at the wrong speed. After a month of hormone treatments and physiotherapy, Uncle Toby showed noticeable, though slow, improvement.

Among his first questions were "What's happening? Why am I in the hospital? Am I ill?" Uncle Toby did not realize that seven years of his life had gone by since he had entered his state of suspended animation. The hospital staff asked him to describe what he had experienced.

"Sort of cool, sort of lazy, slowed down, you know," replied Uncle Toby.

When asked what happened between feeling lazy and being in the hospital, he replied, "Nothing I know of. I suppose I must have . . . passed out, and the family brought me here."

"And how long had you passed out for?" pressed the doctors.
"A day or two—couldn't be any longer."

Uncle Toby had no knowledge that seven years had elapsed. After six weeks of treatment he looked fit and well. Then the unexpected occurred. Uncle Toby began to spit blood. Chest X-rays revealed a massive malignant tumor in his chest. The doctors located X-rays taken seven years earlier and found the beginning of a fast-growing, highly malignant cancer that normally would have been fatal within a few months. Yet Uncle Toby had survived for seven years because of his suspended animation. Survived, that is, until he was warmed up and presumed normal, only to die a few days later. (See *Discover*, February 1988, pp. 56-58.)

♦ ♦ ♦

Strange as it may sound, some teens go through a period in life when they feel like Uncle Toby. They wonder if they have been in a state of suspended animation prior to their rude awakening during adolescence. Childhood is quickly pushed aside by a rush of hormones, feelings, and emotions over which they seem to have little or no control. It seems almost as if they are passing through a time warp. The warm, comfortable security of childhood becomes a distant memory as they are confronted with the new awakenings taking place in their bodies. Strange—almost uncontrollable—forces propel them helter-skelter into relationships and decisions before they are ready.

For a few teens this experience may be nothing more than a gentle shaking from a deep sleep. For others it is like the clanging of a gigantic alarm clock that propels them stumbling and bleary-eyed from their warm bed before they are fully awake. Insecure and confused, they stumble around a strange room (their body) in which the furniture is being rearranged on a daily basis. Life may become a nightmare of fears, fumblings, and frustrations. These teens no longer understand their own actions, desires, or even values. Decisions that used to be so simple, mostly based on their parents' values, become harder to make.

Who am I? is the cry of the insecure teen. What am I doing here? What is my reason for existing? How did I get this way?

Heredity may be a stronger influence on personality traits than either child rearing or family environment.

Two psychologists from the University of Minnesota have offered a partial answer to a teenager's cry for help. In their study of more than 280 pairs of identical and fraternal twins, they found that heredity plays an important role in our actions, thoughts, and even our value systems. They found that heredity may be a stronger influence on personality traits than either child rearing or family environment. (See *USA Today*, Dec. 3, 1986.)

In this ongoing study many of the reunited twins had been separated since birth or shortly thereafter. In fact, most of the twins did not know they were a twin. Not surprisingly, the fraternal twins (not from the same ovum and sperm) did not exhibit common temperament or personality characteristics. However, the identical twins, even though raised in separate environments, still exhibited similar temperaments and personality traits. Even such individual mannerisms as crossing their legs or expressing themselves with their hands tended to be the same with identical twins.

To determine the similarity between twins, Drs. Thomas Bouchard and David Lykken subjected them to 10 days of intensive testing and detailed medical histories. In addition to X-rays, electrocardiograms, heart-stress tests, and other physical testing, the twins were required to answer 15,000 questions, which were fed into a computer for comparison and analysis.

Case A—Male identical twins, aged 39, separated at 37 days. Both twins developed sinus headaches at the age of 10, which turned into migraines during their teen years. They reported similar chest pains and a nervous condition that was treated successfully with Valium. Both engaged in woodworking as a hobby, both worked for a police agency on a volunteer basis, both obtained identical scores on an occupational survey, and both worked at clerical jobs.

The identical twins, even though raised in separate environments, still exhibited similar temperaments and personality traits.

Case B—Male identical twins, aged 24, separated at 5 days. Both were overweight until junior high school, when both became extremely skinny. Both were overt homosexuals, and both developed a fear of heights during childhood. Both had speech problems until the third grade and were hyperactive as children.

Case C—Female identical twins, aged 57, separated at 6 weeks. Both wet the bed until they were age 12-13. Both began experiencing identical nightmares during their teen years, and these dreams continued into their early 40s. They dreamed that doorknobs and fishhooks were being put in their mouths and felt they were being smothered to death.

Case D—Female identical twins, aged 40, separated at 2 weeks. Affectionately dubbed the "giggle sisters" because of their raucous laughter, they walked, talked, and behaved as one. They would each buy the same novel at the same time without the other's knowledge. Their homes were identically decorated (even though they did not know each other previously), and their favorite colors were the same. Even their thought patterns were so identical that one twin would begin a sentence and the other would finish it. *Remember, they had been separated for 40 years, and neither knew she was a twin.*

Your teens have also received inherited tendencies over which they may have little control. These tendencies will become even more evident as they attempt to understand the alien adolescent bodies they now call home.

More than 100 years ago one of my favorite authors made some interesting observations concerning temperament traits: "It will be well to remember that tendencies of character are transmitted from parents to children. . . . In the fear of God gird on the armor for a life conflict with hereditary tendencies" (Ellen G. White, *Testimonies*, vol. 4, p. 439).

"They have not made efforts to correct the objectionable traits of character which were transmitted to them as a birthright" (*ibid.*, p. 323).

"Many children have received as a birthright almost unconquerable tendencies to evil" (Ellen G. White, *The Adventist Home*, p. 256).

"Both parents transmit their own characteristics, mental and physical, their dispositions and appetites, to their children" (Ellen G. White, *Patriarchs and Prophets*, p. 561).

◆ ◆ ◆

The study of human temperaments is much older than these writings from the past century. Approximately 400 years before the birth of Christ, the Greek philosopher and physician Hippocrates wrote extensively on temperaments. Today there are at least 200 different temperament inventories and tests that divide human behavior into four quadrants or areas. The purpose of determining the temperament blends of your teenager children is to increase understanding, tolerance, and patience in your relationship.

Before we examine the four basic temperament types and how they affect your teenagers, let me clarify three words that are often used interchangeably and that sometimes cause confusion.

Temperament—Temperament describes the inborn traits over which we have no control. These traits were given to us by our parents when 23 chromosomes from our mother mingled with 23 chromosomes from our father. Temperament traits are as unpredictable as the color of our eyes, shade of our skin, or any other inherited characteristic. The word "temperament" actually comes from the Latin word *temperare*, which means to mingle. That is precisely what occurs when our mother's and father's chromosomes united and formed a new human being. Since we were not consulted prior to this union, we cannot take credit for the good qualities. Neither should we accept blame for the bad. More about that later.

> **Temperament traits are as unpredictable as the color of our eyes, shade of our skin, or any other inherited characteristic.**

Character—Character is the result of our natural temperaments being modified by everything and everyone that comes in contact with us throughout our lifetimes. Everything we read, watch, speak, think, or do affects our character. There is nothing we can do in life that does not have an influence upon character. Some refer to character as our civilized temperament. Whereas we have no choice over our inherited temperament, we constantly make choices that affect character. Every choice we make (or fail to make) makes an impression on our temperament and shapes our character.

The word "character" is taken from the Latin and refers to an instrument of branding. That accurately describes what we do to our temperaments with every word we speak, every thought we think, every video we watch, every CD we listen to, etc. Every choice we make each day literally *brands* our inherited temperaments to form our characters. In other words, we are in complete control when it comes to character-building.

Personality—Many psychologists use the word "personality" interchangeably with "temperament," which tends to cause some confusion. I believe that the two words have quite different meanings since "personality" comes from the Latin *persona*, which refers to a mask worn by an actor.

> **Everything we read, watch, speak, think, or do affects our character. There is nothing we can do in life that does not have an influence upon character.**

An actor may have many choices as to which mask to wear for a given performance, but we have no choice over our inherited temperament blends. But when it comes to personality, we often find ourselves wearing one "mask" with our friends, a different "mask" with our family, and yet another "mask" for our employer. We have a choice over which mask to wear in almost every situation. Like a true actor, we develop so many masks during a lifetime that it is often difficult to remember who we really are!

The bottom line is that we can choose our personality, but we are stuck with our temperament. That doesn't mean we have no control over our actions. Actually we have a great deal of control as to the feeding and nurturing of our temperaments, unless we have an emotional or mental disorder. The good news is that God knew what He was doing when He gave each person his or her unique temperament blend. That we may be different from everyone else in our immediate family is also God's idea.

"Marked diversities of disposition and character frequently exist in the same family, for it is in the order of God that persons of varied temperament should associate together. When this is the case, each member of the household should sacredly regard the feelings and respect the right of the others. By this means mutual consideration and forbearance will be cultivated, prejudices will be softened, and rough points of character smoothed. Harmony may be secured, and the blending of the varied temperaments may be a benefit to each" (Ellen G. White, *Child Guidance*, p. 205).

I would suggest using the four temperaments as a basis for discovering more about your teenage youngsters and about yourself. Begin by referring to the chart on page 18 for an overview of the basic strengths and weaknesses of each temperament. Although one or more of these temperament types will usually predominate in each person, it cannot fully explain you or your teen. Every person is unique. God seems to use a mold only once! Yet in our uniqueness, God has also placed recognizable similarities. You may find it helpful to make a list of all the traits that apply to you from the temperament chart. Then work together with your teenage children to make a list of all the traits that apply to them. Perhaps you will want to help one another or use a close friend or family member to give each of you insights into your own unique blend. Listen to how your teenagers feel about themselves, and together determine what strengths and weaknesses are inherent in their temperament blends.

> **"Marked diversities of disposition and character frequently exist in the same family, for it is in the order of God that persons of varied temperament should associate together."**

You may find it helpful to divide your lists on separate sheets of paper. On one page you might list traits you admire in yourself or your teen, and on the other page you might include those traits that you would like to see changed.

After you have finished both lists, read them over carefully. Do they accurately represent you and your teenagers? Once you are satisfied with your lists, put the list of admirable qualities for you and your teenagers in a place where you can read over them daily. Crumple up both lists of weaknesses and throw them into the trash can.

Keep in mind that the undesirable traits inherited and those learned are all the result of sin. To be rid of undesirable temperament (inherited) and character (learned) traits is not as easy as throwing a list in the trash can, but it is a way to begin.

"A noble, all-round character is not inherited. It does not come to us by accident. A noble character is earned by individual effort through the merits and grace of Christ. God gives the talents, the powers of the mind; we form the character. . . . Conflict after conflict must be waged against hereditary tendencies. . . . A character formed according to the divine likeness is the only treasure that we can take from this world to the next" (Ellen G. White, *Christ's Object Lessons*, pp. 331, 332).

God gives the talents, the powers of the mind; we form the character.

♦ ♦ ♦

A valid biblical principle that is very important for both you and your teenagers to understand is that *by beholding you become changed*. Spend some time each day reading over your teens' lists of admirable qualities. Watch for those positive qualities and compliment your teenage children whenever these traits appear. Look at your own list each day, and you will also find yourself becoming more and more like the person God intended for you to be. Claim the Bible promise "I can do everything through him who gives me strength" (Phil. 4:13, NIV), and God will help you mold your character around those admirable qualities that He placed in you at conception.

When you find yourself or your teenage children acting out the undesirable traits on the other list, claim another Bible promise: "If we confess our sins, he is faithful and just and will forgive us our sins and purify us from all unrighteousness" (1 John 1:9, NIV). Try this process for 30 days, and see for yourself that it really works!

Temperament Chart

Super Seller
(emotional extrovert)
Lives for the moment!

Strengths
___ Stimulating
___ Personable
___ Enthusiastic
___ Spontaneous
___ Compassionate
___ Dramatic
___ Outgoing
___ Cheerful
___ Friendly
___ Warm
___ Sociable
___ Talkative
___ Carefree
___ Motivating
___ Entertaining
___ TOTAL

Weaknesses
___ Disorganized
___ Forgetful
___ Haphazard
___ Restless
___ Excitable
___ Interrupts
___ Loud
___ Egotistical
___ Self-Centered
___ Unpredictable
___ Exaggerates
___ Show-off
___ Changeable
___ Easily distracted
___ Naive
___ TOTAL

Typical Careers
Public Speaker
Actor/Actress
Salesperson
Preacher
Receptionist
Courtroom Lawyer
Public Relations

Decisive Doer
(unemotional extrovert)
Plans for the future!

Strengths
___ Strong-willed
___ Adventuresome
___ Determined
___ Out-spoken
___ Independent
___ Competitive
___ Visionary
___ Energetic
___ Optimistic
___ Productive
___ Decisive
___ Courageous
___ Leader
___ Organized
___ Focused
___ TOTAL

Weaknesses
___ Crafty
___ Argumentative
___ Unsympathetic
___ Short-Tempered
___ Proud
___ Domineering
___ Sarcastic
___ Inconsiderate
___ Unforgiving
___ Opinionated
___ Workaholic
___ Aggressive
___ Intolerant
___ Revengeful
___ TOTAL

Typical Careers
Entrepreneur
Builder/Contractor
Manager
Executive
President
Crusader
Producer

Timely Thinker
(emotional introvert)
Worries about the past!

Strengths
___ Precise
___ Gifted
___ Analytical
___ Thoughtful
___ Industrious
___ Serious
___ Exacting
___ Orderly
___ Perfectionist
___ Loyal
___ Idealistic
___ Self-sacrificing
___ Creative
___ Self-disciplined
___ Accurate
___ TOTAL

Weaknesses
___ Moody
___ Negative Attitude
___ Rigid
___ Insecure
___ Resentful
___ Dependent
___ Super-sensitive
___ Unforgiving
___ Pessimistic
___ Self-Centered
___ Critical
___ Depressed
___ Skeptical
___ Worrier
___ Hard-to-please
___ TOTAL

Typical Careers
Interior Decorator
Fashion Designer
Author
Professor
Health Care Professional
Musician
Philosopher

Reliable Relater
(unemotional introvert)
Enjoys all of life!

Strengths
___ Calm
___ Quiet
___ Easy-going
___ Listener
___ Practical
___ Supportive
___ Likable
___ Contented
___ Diplomatic
___ Dependable
___ Dry Humor
___ Kindhearted
___ Conservative
___ Neat/organized
___ Patient
___ TOTAL

Weaknesses
___ Stubborn
___ Reluctant
___ Unmotivated
___ Indifferent
___ Uninvolved
___ Conforming
___ Unsure
___ Dependent
___ Compromising
___ Self-protective
___ Doubtful
___ Slow
___ Indecisive
___ Tease
___ Lazy
___ TOTAL

Typical Careers
Accountant
Technician
Diplomat
Teacher
Counselor
Secretary
Administrator

Add the two totals together for each temperament type and record below:

Super Seller _____ Decisive Doer _____ Timely Thinker _____ Reliable Relater _____

CHAPTER 2

Can This Be My Teen?

"When a kid turns 13, stick him in a barrel, nail the lid shut, and feed him through the knothole. When he turns 16, plug the hole."

Mark Twain is reported to have given this unsolicited insight into parent-teen relationships. Have you ever felt that way about your teenage children? Have you ever wondered how they can seemingly read your mind at times and yet be so dense a few moments later? I read that the parents of two teenagers were worried about the failing eyesight of their children. It seems that the daughter couldn't find anything to wear in a closet filled with clothes, and the son couldn't find anything good to eat in a refrigerator full of food.

Actually, you probably know your teenagers well enough to predict with almost uncanny accuracy how they will react before you speak or make your request. This chapter will help you more fully understand your teens, and the next chapter will give you a better understanding of yourself as a parent.

As you begin this study, it is important to know that no teenager is a single temperament type. Each of us is a blend. However, one or two temperament types will usually predominate in one's lifestyle and decision-making. The following temperament types are arranged from the most outgoing (seller) to the most reserved (relater).

SUPER SELLERS' STRENGTHS

Super sellers are energetic, talkative storytellers who live for the moment. They are keenly focused on the present and are usually the life of the party. Sellers exude charisma from every pore of their bodies. Everyone seems to be attracted to them. They have a childlike optimism, always seeing the best in everyone and everything. Sellers appear to be innocent and easily persuaded. They enjoy life and seldom recall the hurts or disappointments of the past.

Sellers exude charisma from every pore of their bodies. Everyone seems to be attracted to them.

Super sellers are constant touchers. In fact, they find it extremely difficult to keep their hands off other people. Super friendly and sincere, these curious teenagers make their way through life good-naturedly bouncing off every obstacle in their way. They make excellent actors, as they are always on stage. They are likely to be envied by those around them, since they apparently enjoy every minute of life. Those brief moments that are not enjoyable are soon forgotten in the thrill of a new moment.

Endowed with tremendous enthusiasm and charm, super sellers are an inspiration to others. In fact, no one will start more projects than a seller. Unfortunately, they seldom finish any of them! The charming super seller makes friends easily and may even be voted the most popular kid in school. However, friends of super sellers should remember this word of caution: No one can love you more—or forget you faster. They thrive on compliments, do not hold grudges, and sincerely love practically everyone. If for some reason super sellers should lose their tempers, they will probably apologize profusely a few minutes later and then take their antagonists out to lunch or invite them to a party.

Decisive Doers' Strengths

You will immediately recognize the strong willpower of decisive doers. Aggressive and future-oriented, they are likely to be workaholics. If it is sports, they will strive to be the best. If it is scholastic achievement, their GPAs will reflect their dogged determination regardless of their IQs. Decisive doers are constantly in motion and never seem to tire. In addition to being self-sufficient and independent, they have a compulsive need to change their environments, along with an urgency to correct all wrongs.

Courageous crusaders, they will probably try to change every perceived unjust rule in school. Born leaders, they are also excellent judges of people (unlike the super sellers, who view everyone through rose-colored glasses). Born with the flame of eternal optimism, fanned by their supreme self-confidence, decisive doers do not know the meaning of the word "defeat." This will be readily apparent on the football field or the school debate team.

> **Doers know only one way to play any game (including the game of life), and that is to *win*.**

Unemotional and goal-oriented, decisive doers let nothing stand between them and success. If you happen to get in their way, *look out*! Great organizers and delegators of work, they are often put in charge of projects that would send lesser persons into spasms of insecurity. Decisive doers thrive on competition and even opposition. Oppose doers, and you will reap the whirlwind. Doers know only one way to play any game (including the game of life), and that is to *win*. Excelling in emergencies, the unemotional decisive doers usually make the right choices and often lead their groups into the winner's circle.

The hard-driving doers seldom have time or need for close friends. Even though they may have many acquaintances and even admirers, they generally use people to accomplish their numerous goals. Those on their "friends" list will often feel both compelled and privileged to help the decisive doers accomplish a worthy task.

Timely Thinkers' Strengths

The sensitive and talented thinkers can be very emotional and are usually in touch with the moods and needs of others. Timely thinkers may be latent geniuses just waiting to be discovered. Serious and purposeful in life, timely thinkers experience both the heights of ecstasy and the pits of despair. Conscientious and idealistic, thinkers strive for perfection in everything they do. Thinkers are loyal, lifelong friends, but they seldom make more than a handful who qualify as their true friends.

Thinkers often consider any grade less than an A as failure.

They are often referred to as "detail hounds" because of their penchant for minute perfection. Timely thinkers' complete attention to detail often drives the fun-loving sellers into temporary exasperation. Thinkers usually feel the need to make certain that every *i* in life is duly dotted.

Timely thinkers are always on time. They follow a schedule and are never late to classes or appointments. Thinkers are orderly, organized, and uncommonly neat. They are consistent and dependable as students or workers. If they major in art, thinkers must wait for the artistic mood to strike before finishing their finest work. If algebra is their specialty, they will burn the midnight oil as they try to solve every equation, with perhaps a few extra for good measure. They love extra credit assignments. If they major in business, the homework must be done before taking time out for recreation. Thinkers do not like to be hurried into doing anything less than a perfect job. In fact, thinkers often consider any grade less than an A as failure.

Content to stay in the background, thinkers make good support partners for doers or sellers, neither of whom can tolerate detail work. Thinkers will listen sympathetically to complaints and exhibit sincere concern for friends and, on occasion, complete strangers. This characteristic is especially important in the normal temperament mix of any family or school organization, since the doers often leave a lot of "walking wounded" in their continual quest for success.

Reliable Relaters' Strengths

The easygoing, witty reliable relaters can see humor in the most mundane situations. Born with a superb sense of timing, relaters can keep you in stitches without ever having to crack a smile. Their low-key personalities wear well, and they are always welcome in a group. Cool, calm, and collected, relaters are dependable and consistent. They usually keep their emotions hidden and are happily reconciled to life. Relaters are supportive as friends and are often considered ideal sons or daughters.

> **Cool, calm, and collected, relaters are dependable and consistent. They usually keep their emotions hidden and are happily reconciled to life.**

Perhaps no one is more dependable during a crisis than reliable relaters. Seldom becoming upset over uncontrollable circumstances, they exercise great patience and calmness when others are losing their minds. They are natural problem-solvers and mediators, who work well under pressure. These traits give relaters natural administrative ability, but they seldom are chosen for that position while in school. Most class elections go to flashy sellers or determined doers. However, later in life relaters may find their natural traits propelling them into the role of administrators or counselors. Always efficient and neat in their chosen areas of interest (otherwise the rest of their lifestyle may resemble a mini-disaster), relaters are valued as friends and confidants.

Thus far we have summarized the basic strengths of the four temperament types. Unfortunately, since sin entered our gene pool in the Garden of Eden, there has also been another side to our temperaments—weaknesses or sinful tendencies.

SUPER SELLERS' WEAKNESSES

Being compulsive talkers, super sellers are often described as entering a room mouth first. In fact, they not only tend to bore others with trivia, but often cannot remember names and constantly exaggerate when telling their favorite stories. Their happy-go-lucky attitude may cause others to distrust them because they seem phony or untrustworthy. Their loud voices and blustery complaints can be an embarrassment at times. Superegotistical, the obnoxious sellers love to talk about themselves. Emotionally unstable, sellers cry almost as easily as they laugh. In fact, they may switch so rapidly from expressing anger to seeking forgiveness that they appear out of control and insincere to both doers and thinkers.

Their motto: If it feels good, do it!

As those who would rather talk than work, sellers are also weak-willed and undisciplined. Their motto: If it feels good, do it! Although their minds are usually filled with hundreds of ideas, they are often disasters when it comes to implementing those ideas. They tend to forget obligations, appointments, assignments, and resolutions on account of the distractions of the "moment." Unfortunately, super sellers seldom live up to their potential or others' expectations.

Unable to determine their own limitations, sellers often bite off more than they can chew. When asked to do something, their usual response is yes. However, time-wasting habits and their lack of organization, combined with their uncontrollable tendency to say yes, make sellers candidates for failure unless they learn self-control, the basic success ingredient often missing in their lives. Because they are so easily distracted, they find it difficult to set or maintain priorities. Although they always intend to do the right thing, they just never seem to get around to it. That's why a seller can have an IQ of 140 and a C average in school.

Sellers need both a stage and an audience. They hate to be alone, and expect everyone they meet to like them. They want to get credit (even if it isn't due them), and become sullen if slighted. They tend to dominate a conversation, fail to listen (since they are too busy preparing their next monologue), answer questions before they are asked, give answers for others, or interrupt and repeat their stories ad nauseam. Add to this list fickleness and forgetfulness, as well as a tendency to make excuses for their failures, and you have a fair picture of super sellers' weaknesses.

> **Doers enjoy controversy and arguments. They do not know how to lose gracefully.**

Decisive Doers' Weaknesses

Decisive doers have the reputation for being bossy, arrogant, impatient, quick-tempered, explosive, and grudge-bearing. It has been said that doers will have an ulcer before they are 40 and will have given ulcers to 40 others (including their parents) by that time. They often launch programs that they later regret, but their pride will not let them admit a mistake and start over. Because of their tenacity to hang in there, even after they should have let go, they often succeed, but sometimes at a terrible cost to themselves and others.

Doers enjoy controversy and arguments. Since they do not know how to lose gracefully (or any other way, for that matter), they play to win. This usually limits their friends to those who can overlook their competitive nature or who will receive some benefit from the friendship. Doers despise those who cry or show their emotions, even though they display the emotion of anger repeatedly. Lacking a sense of sensitivity, they see expressed emotions as a sign of weakness. Self-sufficient, haughty, and proud, doers can be extremely obnoxious and quite unsympathetic.

Often in charge of the class annual or newspaper, doers have little tolerance for mistakes. Bored by trivia, many times they fail to read instructions and sometimes make hasty decisions based on insufficient data. Once made, however, these decisions are cast in concrete and will be defended until death. Although they are often rude and tactless, doers can be very charming when it is to their advantage. Unlike sellers, who tend to use things to influence people, doers use people to accomplish things. In addition, Doers expect—and often demand—complete loyalty and obedience.

Timely thinkers find it very difficult to forget the past and plan for the future.

Decisive doers also have an irritating tendency to make decisions for others and without their consent. Since they usually feel they have superior knowledge in the matter (even if they don't), they feel justified in making such decisions. Also, they tend to be very possessive of anything that they consider their personal property. This may even include friends. Because they lack the ability to pronounce the s word (sorry), it's difficult for them to apologize. They may exhibit the same reluctance to show approval. These characteristics make doers unpopular and even feared by those who know them well.

TIMELY THINKERS' WEAKNESSES

Timely thinkers find it very difficult to forget the past and plan for the future. They are extremely sensitive and often take offense when none is intended. Thinkers find it especially difficult to deal with anger and frustration.

I have often compared thinkers to cows chewing their cuds. One of the more memorable things from my childhood involved watching my father's cows eat. I soon learned that when a cow chews her cud, it means she is actually eating her food more than once. Since a cow has a number of stomachs that contain food in various stages of digestion, she burps up the food she has already eaten, chews on it awhile, and then swallows it once more. A cow does this repeatedly until all her food is fully digested.

Thinkers follow the same procedure when dealing with anger or frustration. Rather than confront the source of their anger directly, they swallow hard and walk away. But later, when they are alone, they "burp up" the incident, recall it in living color, and get angry all over again. This procedure may continue almost indefinitely until their anger is finally resolved. Eventually some unlucky person will come into their presence just after the thinker has "burped," and this hapless individual will receive the full fury of undigested wrath!

Thinkers confront the source of their anger directly, they swallow hard and walk away.

It may sound strange, but thinkers actually seem to enjoy playing the martyr. Perhaps because they often have a low self-image, they may feel more comfortable in the martyr's role as their inevitable and just reward in life. While this role may make them appear humble to others, thinkers may actually possess a false sense of humility based upon their proud perfectionism. In other words, since thinkers cannot live up to their own expectations (neither can anyone else), they appear humble to others. This tendency may make thinkers very demanding as work superintendents or parents.

Thinkers often suffer from guilt . . . Guilt . . . GUILT! They may even have a persecution complex. Thinkers tend to develop a rather pessimistic attitude. Their constant self-examination may turn them into hypochondriacs, finding illness and symptoms where none really exist.

Whether at home, school, or work, thinkers prefer to work alone. They often seek out a little corner to themselves rather than be in the middle of a busy room. Once they find a secluded spot, they can accomplish much. Not afraid to tackle difficult assignments, thinkers are a definite plus to any school or organization, as long as they are not in constant contact with people.

They also prefer analysis rather than busy work. Thinkers need to know that what they are doing is important and makes a difference. However, they do not desire the spotlight, as they would rather be support persons who produce high-quality work. Even though they are often difficult to please, their high standards enable them to produce superior work. Thinkers must constantly be reassured that they are truly appreciated. A solid compliment each day will motivate them to greater levels of productivity.

In social circles, thinkers may appear somewhat withdrawn and even remote. They tend to live their lives vicariously—through others. Thinkers usually date and eventually marry a seller or a doer. Born with suspicious natures, thinkers often hold back affection and inwardly resent opposition. Even though they desire and need compliments, thinkers are often skeptical and may impute ulterior motives when they receive a compliment.

Relaters often lack motivation, enthusiasm, and decision-making skills.

RELIABLE RELATERS' WEAKNESSES

Reliable relaters openly display very few weaknesses because of their charming personalities and easygoing lifestyles. Unlike the more visible doers or sellers, they are more reserved, and one must look deeper and longer to determine the effects of sin in this temperament. Relaters often lack motivation, enthusiasm, and decision-making skills. They frequently do not like to get involved. They also tend to avoid responsibility, and can be as stubborn as a

Missouri mule. Although they're often viewed as shy and retiring, no one can be more set in his or her ways or more self-righteous. Often seen as compromising, relaters are actually peace-loving individuals who dislike confrontations of any sort.

Because they lack motivation, relaters may depend on others to point out their tasks or work assignments. While this works quite well in the predictable structure of a classroom, it may become a problem later in life as they enter the workplace. Some refer to relaters as the original energy conservationists! No one can conserve energy better than relaters, especially if it is their own! They actually resent being pushed into any work assignment that was not their idea to begin with. Viewed as somewhat careless and lazy, their laid-back attitudes may be sources of irritation or even discouragement for roommates or friends.

While relaters tend to be somewhat unexciting as friends, their dry sense of humor keeps them in demand. However, their tendency to tease and judge in jest can sometimes strain difficult relationships. Usually attracted to sellers or doers, they may frustrate their more progressive companions with their tendency to resist change or not to accept new ideas and concepts.

In this brief review of the four temperaments you have probably found your teenagers, spouse, and a few good friends. Hopefully you have gained some insights into yourself at the same time. It is important to state again that no one has a single temperament type. Therefore, when discussing temperaments or analyzing your teenage children, do not expect them to fit neatly into one classification

> **No one can conserve energy better than relaters, especially if it is their own! They actually resent being pushed into any work assignment that was not their idea to begin with.**

or another. This knowledge of inherited tendencies will be useful as you attempt to understand yourself, your teenagers, and others.

Body Types and Temperament Types

Some studies have reported research on various body types that might also prove helpful in trying to understand your teenage children. While much in this field of study is anecdotal or speculative, the following information may prove entertaining even if it does lack scientific agreement.

Super sellers often possess what is called the G type body. The chest predominates, since the heart and lungs need air and space (remember, sellers enter a room mouth-first). Their upper bodies are often a full size smaller than below the waist, which gives them somewhat of a pyramid appearance. They tend to like spicy, creamy foods that stimulate their sex glands (just what you wanted to hear as a parent!). Their favorite facial expression tends to be lively, and they are great improvisers.

While body types may not specifically identify your teens' behaviors, they may provide insights into their temperament blends.

Decisive doers' bodies are often dominated by bones and muscle. As born leaders, their type A body is often stocky or full-figured. They are high-energy people who tend to stimulate the adrenal gland with salty food or red meat (if vegetarian, I suppose they eat kidney beans!). Their facial expressions tend to be more severe, even though, like sellers, they are active and easily excited.

Timely thinkers may have bodies dominated by the head and nervous system. Known as the T type body, they tend to have full hips and thighs with slender appendages (arms and legs). To activate the thyroid gland, they prefer sweets and starches. Their sensitive natures may lead to a nervous condition or even depression at times. Their facial expressions are often anxious or stressful.

Reliable relaters' bodies are often dominated by their digestive system (isn't that a pleasant thought?). Even though they usually eat rather slowly, their digestive system is often troubled. Their P type body may have baby fat and small feet. They tend to eat dairy products to stimulate the pituitary gland. Their generally passive nature is mirrored through their calm and serene facial expression.

While body types may not specifically identify your teens' behaviors, they may provide insights into their temperament blends. As you observe your teen children's facial expressions, it will help you understand their underlying agenda and temperament traits. You might want to use body types as a discussion tool after supper some night—just for fun!

Unfortunately, as sinful human beings, we all share a common problem that must not be overlooked in our quest for understanding. "Our natural tendencies, unless corrected by the Holy Spirit of God, have in them the seeds of moral death" (Ellen G. White, *The Ministry of Healing*, p. 455).

> **"Our natural tendencies, unless corrected by the Holy Spirit of God, have in them the seeds of moral death."**

Jesus reminded Nicodemus (and us): "Truly, truly, I say to you, unless one is born anew, he cannot see the kingdom of God" (John 3:3, RSV). It is important for us to realize that even though we were born with the seeds of moral death already within us, God has provided a solid solution to our dilemma. "There is therefore now no condemnation for those who are in Christ Jesus" (Rom. 8:1, RSV).

Isn't that good news! It might even make your day. I know it makes mine every time I read it. However, this good news does not excuse our bad behavior. It was meant to change our behavior!

"A noble, all-round character is not inherited. It does not come to us by accident. A noble character is earned by individual effort through the merits and grace of Christ. God gives the talents, the powers of the mind; we form the character. . . . Conflict after conflict must be waged against hereditary tendencies. . . . A character formed according to the divine likeness is the only treasure that we can take from this world to the next" (*Christ's Object Lessons*, pp. 331, 332).

Our transformation of character does not change our temperament blend, but transforms the temperaments we were given at birth.

"Man is not endowed with new faculties, but the faculties he has are sanctified." "The natural inclinations are softened and subdued. New thoughts, new feelings, new motives are implanted. A new standard of character is set up—the life of Christ" (Ellen G. White, in *Review and Herald*, July 7, 1904).

The good news is that Jesus came to amplify (turn up the volume of) our God-given strengths and to cancel out (like a Dolby brand noise reducer on a high-fidelity stereo) our sinful tendencies. Remember Paul's desperate cry for help: "Wretched man that I am! Who will deliver me from this body of death?" (Rom. 7:24, RSV). Never forget his answer: "Thanks be to God through Jesus Christ our Lord! . . . There is therefore now no condemnation for those who are in Christ Jesus" (Rom. 7:25-8:1, RSV).

It is not our temperament blend that causes problems; it is sin that has attached itself like a parasite.

As you review your own temperament blend and that of your teenagers, with all their strengths and weaknesses, remember that Jesus came to make *both of you* into a new creation. During this restoration process He does not eliminate the identification marks of your unique temperament blend. Instead He preserves everything about your temperament blend that is inherently good and seeks to eliminate those areas created by sin.

When we are born again, our temperaments will surely be altered, but we will not change temperaments. God had a particular temperament blend in mind for you and perhaps another for your children. It is not our temperament blend that causes problems; it is sin that has attached itself like a parasite. This parasite of unwanted tendencies is transmitted from generation to generation. The good news is that God promises to remove that parasite from both you and your teen so completely that it is even removed from your computer disk in heaven (1 John 1:9).

Once we are born again, the need to use a persona (mask) slowly diminishes as Jesus begins the restoration work in our lives. It becomes less and less necessary to cover up our real selves. The character change that begins inside us eventually manifests itself in our outward actions. Therefore, as we grow in Christ, there are fewer sinful parasites to hide, and more of the inner beauty God originally designed begins to shine through.

Thinkers invent a product that is manufactured by doers and later sold by sellers to be enjoyed by relaters.

Again I want to emphasize that no one is a single temperament. None of us fits neatly into a single temperament type. We are all unique blends. The laws of genetics estimate that the chances of two people being exactly alike are about 1 in 300 billion. So even though we can identify general characteristics and similarities in each temperament type, no one fits neatly into that package, including your offspring. However, a general knowledge about temperament types should help you better understand your own actions as well as those of everyone around you.

To paraphrase Florence Littauer, remember temperament strengths this way: Thinkers invent a product that is manufactured by doers and later sold by sellers to be enjoyed by relaters. Temperament weaknesses may be summarized in this manner:

Sellers enjoy people and forget them; thinkers are annoyed by people, but let them go their own way; doers use people to accomplish their goals and afterward ignore them; relaters study people with haughty indifference.

Adolescence is an unsettled time at best for your teenagers, so I would urge you to use this knowledge to make all of you more aware of your strengths and weaknesses. In addition, knowledge of temperament types should make you more understanding and tolerant of your friends and family as well as your teenagers.

As you are filled with God's Spirit, you will become even more aware of that cancerous malignancy of sin dwelling within. But the good news is that Jesus is working right now to remove that malignancy and make you whole again. Claim this precious promise whenever you sense that sin has taken over your body: "If we confess our sins, he is faithful and just, and will forgive our sins and cleanse us from all unrighteousness" (1 John 1:9, RSV).

Another promise worthy of memorization and daily recall is: "For whatever is born of God overcomes the world [sinful tendencies]; and this is the victory that overcomes the world [sinful tendencies], our faith. Who is it that overcomes the world [sinful tendencies] but he who believes that Jesus is the Son of God?" (1 John 5:4, 5, RSV).

Claim these promises daily, and be all that God intended for you to be in Christ Jesus!

CHAPTER 3

Is This Really Me?

Grandmother was putting her little granddaughter to bed one evening when the child remarked, "Mommy and Daddy are entertaining some very important people downstairs."

Amazed at the little girl's insight, Grandmother agreed. "That's right, honey, but how did you know they were important?"

"That's easy," replied the little girl. "Mommy's laughing at all of Daddy's jokes."

Does that sound familiar in your family? Do you put on a good facade in front of your friends or important business associates, only to return to your normal self the next morning at the breakfast table?

Now that you have discovered your teen children's temperament blends, why not use this knowledge to discover yourself as well? Take a moment to review the temperament chart on page 18, keeping in mind that no one is a single temperament and that everyone is a blend of temperaments. You will probably discover some predominant temperament characteristics that will help you understand yourself.

In this chapter we shall use the four basic temperament types to explain why people parent the way they do. As you consider yourself and your loved ones, don't forget to look for the one or two temperament types that are most noticeable in their personalities. As you study your parenting style, remember the words that a little girl wrote in an essay on the topic of parents: "We got our parents so late in age that it's impossible to change their habits." Although that is not entirely true, it is difficult to change inherited traits.

SUPER SELLER PARENTS

Super sellers are most likely to be voted Parent of the Year by their peers and every teen in the neighborhood. Seller parents make a tremendous first impression and love to tell stories and spend time with younger people. Sellers are often referred to as having a Santa Claus personality. While this seems good on the surface, it has underlying problems. Seller parents desperately want to be liked and will often become permissive, more intent on being liked than disciplining.

> **"We got our parents so late in age that it's impossible to change their habits."**

Seller parents will often disappear when a distasteful task is at hand. I must confess that I managed to avoid the unpleasant task of changing our son's diapers. It wasn't easy, and I took a lot of kidding, but it seemed a small price to pay at the time. Especially when I considered the alternative!

Seller parents will often take over at their teenagers' parties. Sellers love to be the center of attention and will probably be well-liked by the teens, but at the same time their behavior may spark some jealousy pangs in their own children. In fact, sellers may overshadow their teens so completely that the kids both love and resent their super seller parent(s) at the same time. Seller parents love to work with young people. It helps sellers maintain a youthful posture and provides the kind of fast-paced activity they really enjoy.

Being a seller parent myself, I was deeply involved in working with Pathfinders (a program similar to Scouting), and I probably enjoyed it even more than the kids. I lived, ate, and breathed Pathfindering to the point that my wife felt neglected. This sort of dedication can cause serious problems in a marital relationship. If one parent is a seller, the other parent may slip into occasional periods of depression, resulting in the accusation "You'd rather spend your time with _____ than me!"

Seller parents are constantly looking for an audience that has not heard all their stories. Their immediate family has probably heard them so often that they can repeat them all from memory. Seller parents realize that fact and may appear somewhat withdrawn in casual conversation at home. At times they may even seem preoccupied. But in the presence of visitors or strangers, *look out!* Seller parents suddenly come alive and make a big hit with everyone.

> **Sellers are often more spontaneous with visitors than with family, not because the family is unimportant, but because they've already heard everything sellers have to say ad nauseam.**

Teens often resent this apparent Jekyll-and-Hyde behavior because sellers seldom show such enthusiasm when they are with them. It isn't until sellers are confronted with a fresh audience that they suddenly become Personality Plus. Sellers are often more spontaneous with visitors than with family, not because the family is unimportant, but because they've already heard everything sellers have to say ad nauseam.

If you are married to a seller, try to supply a fresh audience every few weeks and then join in on the fun.

Another trait that some (especially thinkers) may find particularly distasteful is seller parents' tendencies to exaggerate. They tend to talk in colorful extremes with little attention to detail. They feel that stories are a lot like sandwiches—without a little dressing, they're dry and get stuck in the throat. What they refer to as a little dressing others might call an outright lie. However, constantly correcting sellers will cause them to withdraw from your presence. Try to understand that they are not intentionally changing the facts; it is merely their nature to exaggerate them in order to embellish the story and make it more dramatic.

> **They tend to talk in colorful extremes with little attention to detail. They feel that stories are a lot like sandwiches—without a little dressing, they're dry and get stuck in the throat.**

Perhaps the following suggestions will help both spouse and teens relate to seller parents. First of all, accept the fact that while they are truly idea persons, they probably are not very good at carrying out their ideas. Sellers may be great starters but are often poor finishers. In field and track they would likely run the 100-yard dash very well, but be much less competent in the mile and a complete disaster in a marathon.

In many ways seller parents are an adult version of immature teenagers. They go through life enjoying the moment, oblivious to any future consequences.

Seller parents thrive on variety. They are easily bored with routine and may even be job-hoppers. They will often talk about a great new opportunity that is about to come their way. Also they will often promise more than they can deliver. Sellers aren't intentionally deceptive, but they will usually say yes under the pressure of the moment. Unfortunately, yes may apply only to that very moment and not the future. Seller parents live in the present, and when they answer yes, they sincerely mean it . . . at that moment. They truly intend to carry out what they have promised, but unfortunately there are so many people to whom they have answered yes that there isn't enough time to fulfill all their promises. Thus the most recent yes often takes precedence over a previous yes from the more distant past (such as an hour earlier).

Be aware that seller parents are often controlled by circumstances. Like chameleons, they are greatly influenced by their surroundings. Their moods and emotions will frequently depend on those around them. Most of sellers' decisions are based upon their immediate feelings rather than a careful analysis of the facts. This is important information for both spouses and teens to understand and remember!

Finally, seller parents live for words of praise. In fact, if an affirmation is not frequently forthcoming, they will often

> **Timing is vitally important if one expects seller parents to accept criticism. Even then it will be difficult for them to hear anything other than a compliment.**

fish for one by asking leading questions. I always ask my wife to comment on my speaking right after I finish a seminar. She has learned not to share any criticism with me at that time, because all I really want then is a compliment. The rest of the story (the true critique) can come later when I am more emotionally detached from my presentation.

Understand that timing is vitally important if one expects seller parents to accept criticism. Even then it will be difficult for them to hear anything other than a compliment. Seller parents complimented daily are usually happy parents. Seller parents enjoy receiving compliments as much as receiving presents, and they can never get too many. This is also true of seller teens. Try it! It will do wonders for your relationship with your seller teenage children and also give you valuable experience in relating to your other seller friends.

A family in the East was planning a month's vacation to the West Coast. At the last minute seller Dad's work prevented him from going, but thinker Mom insisted that she was capable of driving, and they were not going to cancel the trip. Like a true thinker she labored over the road maps, planned their complete route, decided how far they would travel each day, and made motel reservations for the entire trip.

A couple of weeks later seller Dad completed his work assignment earlier than expected and decided to fly out to the West Coast to surprise his family. Because thinker Mom had mapped out their entire vacation route, he knew where they would be each day. So without phoning to tell them he was coming, seller Dad flew out to the West Coast city where they were staying and took a taxi out into the country on a highway that, according to thinker Mom's travel plan, the family should be traveling on later that day. The surprised taxi driver dropped the insistent parent off by the side of the road, and seller Dad settled down to wait for the family car.

> **Decisive doers are perhaps the most responsible parents, but may well be the most difficult to relate to emotionally.**

Soon he spotted the car and stuck out his thumb as his family approached. "Hey, wasn't that Dad?" yelled one of the kids. Thinker Mom did a double take, slammed on the brakes, and backed up to pick up the familiar hitchhiker.

Later, when a newspaper reporter asked the man why he would do such a crazy thing, he responded, "After I die, I want my kids to be able to say, 'Dad sure was a lot of fun, wasn't he?'"

DECISIVE DOER PARENTS

Decisive doers are perhaps the most responsible parents, but may well be the most difficult to relate to emotionally. Doer parents usually have the correct answer for every problem and can often persuade everyone that they are knowledgeable on a topic even if they cannot pronounce the name. Doers will set goals for everyone in their family, as well as daily work schedules. Woe unto the family member who fails to accomplish an assignment!

One thing about doer parents is that they are usually consistent. They will never leave a teen stranded at school or promise to be somewhere and not show up. If they cannot attend a function, they will tell you in advance. Directness is a way of life for doer parents. As Oprah Winfrey would say, they cut to the chase—or get to the bottom line very quickly.

Being relatively unemotional, they often consider crying a form of weakness. This is especially true if doer parents happen to be male. Whereas they may tolerate some crying from a daughter, they probably will not accept it from a son. Doer parents may even encourage teens to keep most of their emotions hidden. Especially the emotions normally associated with tenderness and sympathy.

Doer parents have one driving emotion—*anger*. Actually, doer parents are constantly driven by the emotion of anger. It is inner rage that drives them to be extremely competitive. Even when relaxing, doer parents are intense. If they invite their teenage children to play a game of tennis, they will employ power serves and lots of grunts. There is only one way they can play a game—to *win*! This applies to all areas of life for doer parents. Until they are filled with the Holy Spirit, controlling this inner anger may be an almost insurmountable task.

Doer parents are usually very domineering and control the family with an iron hand. Whether father or mother, doer parents will be the decision-makers in the household. The family soon learns to wear a submissive mask when in their presence. Teens and spouses often learn to suppress their real feelings and stifle their true temperaments in order to prevent strife at home.

Often children of doer parents will grow up displaying a high degree of thinker or relater temperament traits even though they may really be sellers or doers. Such adaptation is often necessary for peace (or even survival) and may not truly represent their God-given temperament blend. When such repression is recognized and teenagers understand their real temperament blend, it is often like setting a prisoner free.

Often children of doer parents will grow up displaying a high degree of thinker or relater temperament traits even though they may really be sellers or doers.

If you are a doer parent, it may be necessary for you to suppress your natural tendencies temporarily so that your teens can be the persons they truly are.

Doer parents also tend to be workaholics. Their idea of love is to provide well and make the family proud of their accomplishments, whether it be in home, hobby, or career. Indolence or idleness will not be tolerated. According to doer parents, productivity is next to godliness. It is often with a sigh of relief that the family waves goodbye to a doer parent leaving on a business trip. Even family vacations can be a time of stress if the doer parent does not learn to relax or at least to allow the rest of the family to do so.

Doer parents are usually impatient when trying to instruct

teenagers. Often they will impatiently snatch a project from a teen's fumbling fingers, accompanied by one (or all) of the following comments: "Can't you do anything right?" "How many times do I have to tell you?" "Are you so thickheaded you can't understand anything?"

Doer parents expect both conformity and excellence from all family members. The tragedy of this expectation is that they may become convinced that teenagers are worthless or at least inept and subject them to verbal ridicule on a daily basis. Doer parents may cause their teen offspring to experience a multitude of confusing feelings during adolescent years. Such confused feelings may alternate between love and hate or admiration and loathing.

I would not want the reader to think that doer parents are the only cause of teen rebellion. Teenagers' own temperaments play an important role, as well as their peer group and other circumstances. Yet doer parents are sometimes the catalyst that ignites this rebellion. It is not uncommon for thinker teens of doer parents to be depressed. In fact, the domineering stance of the doers may cause even bubbly seller teens to slip into depression on occasion.

> **Doer parents expect both conformity and excellence from all family members.**

Sometimes the children of doer parents have not been allowed to fail or make their own decisions. This only adds additional fuel to the rebellion fires that sometimes burn during the teen years. Quite simply, if teens have never been allowed to make decisions for fear that they might make a mistake, they are not equipped to make the life-changing decisions of an emerging adult.

All right! You've heard enough. You admit it. You are a doer parent. Now what? First of all, try to understand your almost obsessive need to be in control.

Doers have a God-given ability to provide logical answers to complex problems. Teens may not always like those answers, but doers will usually be right. Because doers have the ability to provide simple solutions to seemingly complex problems, teens may resent the candor and ease with which the solution is suggested.

Not being diplomatic is one of doer parents' greatest mistakes. So rather than trying to move immovable objects, why not learn how to listen and understand so that you are not distracted by your own anger? Who knows, you might even benefit from your teens' feedback if your feelings do not get in the way.

Doer parents can be impatient with everyone, not just their immediate family. Doers seem to have a definite gift for making others miserable if they do not perform according to doers' expectations or timetables.

Once you have asked Christ to take control of you, ask Him to teach you to speak respectfully, without an argumentative tone.

So as a doer, learn to listen . . . Listen . . . LISTEN. Learn how to bend and compromise on issues that are not life-threatening or moral decisions. It may be difficult to change, but with the infilling of God's Spirit it is not only possible, but a promise: "I can do everything God asks me to with the help of Christ who gives me the strength and power" (Phil. 4:13, TLB).

Once you have asked Christ to take control of you, ask Him to teach you to speak respectfully, without an argumentative tone. Learn not to interrupt. Learn how to listen intently (and show it with your body language). In other words, wait until your teenagers are finished speaking before proclaiming your pronouncements. If after hearing out your teens completely, you still think your solution is better or requires further explanation, allow some time to pass before you confront them again. This will allow your teenage children to absorb the conversation. It also gives the impression that you have spent some time seriously considering the matter yourself.

Understand that doer parents live their lives according to definite plans and goals. They view last-minute adjustments to "perfect" plans as inconsiderate and disruptive. When teens shirk their responsibilities, they cannot expect doer parents to offer a sympathetic ear.

Doer parents may be firm, but they are usually fair. However, doers are not filled with compassion, and thus react negatively to a sob story. They somehow feel that uncontrolled emotions and circumstances are for the weak and unsuccessful. Doers cannot identify with hurt feelings, so it is usually a waste of time trying invoke their sympathy. They deal with the nitty-gritty of everyday reality, not with the philosophical posturing of "what if" or with the terrible tears of a pity party.

> **Doer parents may be firm, but they are usually fair. However, doers are not filled with compassion, and thus react negatively to a sob story.**

Finally, the tongue is often doer parents' worst enemy. No one can be more cutting, critical, or sarcastic than doers. Yet they really don't intend to be sarcastic or offend others. It is just one of those sinful tendencies that they will often spend a lifetime fighting, unless they allow God to give them the victory.

The bottom line in dealing with doers is to speak directly and respectfully. Doer parents may have rough exteriors, but they can be counted on when there is a genuine need.

I am reminded of the teenagers of a very prominent family who decided to give their doer father a book of the family's history for a birthday present. Knowing how their father did not like to be reminded of any "weak branches" in their family tree, they commissioned a professional biographer to do the work, carefully warning him of the family's "black sheep" problem.

It seems that Uncle George had been executed in the electric chair for murder. The tactful biographer (a relater) assured the worried teens, "I can handle that situation so that there will be absolutely no cause for embarrassment."

When the children received the final draft of their family history, Uncle George's past read like this: "Uncle George occupied a chair of applied electronics at an important government institution. He was attached to his position by the strongest of ties, and his death came as a real shock."

Timely Thinker Parents

Thinker parents often have artistic inclinations as well as tremendous intellectual capabilities. Thinkers often insist that their teens take music lessons even if they have no talent or desire in that area.

I remember how hard we tried to persuade our son to develop his musical ability. Being a seller/relater, he really had very little interest in pursuing music. He tried to placate Mom and Dad by trying guitar, trumpet, and voice, but soon he lost interest in each one. Thinker parents are often confused as to why their offspring don't share their interest in the arts.

I know a thinker parent who limited his own career in order to provide proper musical training for his talented daughter. She was a very gifted thinker, and her father recognized that her raw God-given talent needed proper direction and honing if she was to develop it fully. He decided that before accepting an invitation to work in a particular area (even if it meant a promotion) he would first check to see if there was a suitable instructor for his daughter.

His vision was for her to become a concert pianist. Not only did he provide her with the best instructors, but he also spent time every day listening to her practice. Today she is an accomplished concert pianist, thanks to the dedication of her thinker father.

Thinkers may not understand that teenage children do not necessarily share their enthusiasm for artistic ability or even taste. If their teenagers don't take to music lessons, thinker parents will often lament, "Where did I fail you?" and go through life feeling like a failure as a parent.

Thinker parents also tend to set very high standards for their teenage youngsters' behavior, school grades, hobbies, sports, or almost anything else teens might do. If their teens do not happen to share these high standards, it will often send thinker parents into a whirlpool of self-pity or even depression. Such displays may foster guilt feelings in their teenage offspring and often compel the troubled teenagers to try to please their parents or feel that they are failures because of their apparent lack of accomplishments.

Thinker parents mean well and just want their teens to excel in whatever they do. Unfortunately, sometimes it is more for the sake of the thinker parents themselves than for their children. The key word in a thinker's lifestyle is "quality." Thinkers expect their teens to agree that quality is more important than quantity. This pressure creates a dilemma for seller or doer teenagers, who have other priorities.

The key word in a thinker's lifestyle is "quality."

Thinker parents often rush their teenage children into adulthood. Because thinkers often marry doers, apparent child prodigies are often pushed along in school by their success-oriented parents. Thinker parents often feel inferior and may attempt to live out their lives through their children. Such feelings of inferiority often cause thinker parents to clash with seller teens, who seem too frivolous and do not take life seriously. Likewise they create stress for themselves by trying to convince doer teens that quality is more important than quantity. Whereas relater teens will not usually confront their parents, they may be a constant source of worry for thinker parents because of their apparent lack of motivation.

Thinker parents often suffer through periodic bouts of depression, many times compounded with a deep-seated martyr complex. Thinkers often use guilt as their main weapon to control their teenage young people. Thinker parents may subtly remind their teenagers how much they have done for them and conclude with "And this is all the thanks I get?" Occasionally thinker parents may act more like undercover martyrs who pour out their lives for their teens, giving them everything they desire. This may result in thinker parents becoming personal servants to their teens. Such a situation is unhealthy for both. Such actions may eventually cause guilt on a subconscious level, and unsuspecting teens may spend the rest of their lives trying to repay their thinker parents, without ever really knowing why. If the teenagers are doers, they may well understand the dynamic that is happening and happily use their parents to get what they want.

Thinkers are masters of nonverbal communication.

Thinker parents are second only to doer parents when it comes to ruling with an iron hand. Thinkers are masters of nonverbal communication. They can often devastate teenagers with a roll of the eyes, a deep sigh, a hurt look, or silence. Thinker mothers may control their teens with a slight tear or deep, heart-wrenching sobs. When they reach their late teens or adulthood, many young people grow to resent such obvious manipulation. Sadly, those who do not see through this manipulation may pass on to their own children these codependency traits and attitudes.

It is helpful to understand the sensitive nature of thinker parents. They are easily hurt and can brood for weeks over a real or imagined slight. Without meaning to or even realizing it, doer or seller teenagers can easily offend thinker parents. Something teens might say in a joking manner is often taken seriously, and the parents feel offended when no offense was intended. On the positive side, thinkers can understand their teens when they are in the pits of despair.

Thinker parents are born with a basically pessimistic nature. They can always discern the problems in any endeavor, but they have difficulty seeing the possibilities. This can be very discouraging to teens in their idealistic years. The clash of pessimistic parents and optimistic teenagers can be very disruptive to the family. The key for thinker parents is to listen to their teens and refrain from ridiculing their idealistic view of the world around them. Remember that in any conversation between parents and teens, the truth is often found somewhere between the opposing points of view. It is a sign of maturity to listen and modify one's own thinking, even if it disagrees with one's basic nature or presuppositions.

Fear and insecurity are constant companions of thinker parents. Thinkers tend to overprotect their teenage children because of their own fears and insecurities. They may even come between teens and their friends in an effort to protect them from bad influences. While this may be necessary in some instances, it can build a wall between parents and teens. This wall may be built by the parents' basic insecurity, rather than the teens' "bad" company. If deprived of peer friendships, some teens will rebel or perhaps become fearful of making decisions on their own.

Thinkers tend to overprotect their teenage children because of their own fears and insecurities.

Thinkers tend to make "mountains out of molehills." Because thinker parents worry a lot, it is important that they teach their children to keep them informed of their whereabouts long before they become teenagers. All parents should require their teens to keep them informed as to where they are going and when they will arrive home. It is but common courtesy for family members to call when they are delayed and give an approximate time of arrival.

Teens taught this basic courtesy early in life will find it much easier to function later as spouses or parents.

RELIABLE RELATER PARENTS

The stabilizing influence in a family is often the relater parent. Relaters thrive on routine. Their schedule seldom varies. While this may bring needed order and security into the lives of little children, it can be extremely boring to teenagers. However, it is comforting to know that relater parents seldom get rattled or even irritated by adolescent behavior. They are able to maintain a calm and accepting attitude even when confronted with the most unpleasant circumstances or obnoxious young people.

> **The stabilizing influence in a family is often the relater parent. Relaters thrive on routine. Their schedule seldom varies.**

Because relater parents genuinely value relationships above all else, they avoid conflict at all costs. While this may seem desirable at first glance, it soon gives relaters the reputation of being wimps or doormats. Even though struggling teenagers may not want to think such thoughts about their parents, it may occur to them that one parent is constantly dominating the other. Teenage youngsters do not understand that this is often the choice of the relater parent, who prefers to leave discipline and confrontation to the more outgoing seller or doer.

My wife is a thinker/relater, and she tries to avoid confrontation whenever possible. Since I am a seller/doer, I usually became the heavy whenever discipline or confrontation was necessary in our family. I remember one time when she placed our son, Mitch, in a corner to await my return to the house. The idea was for me to administer the discipline and confront his unacceptable behavior.

We were visiting my parents on their farm, and my father and I were finishing the chores when this incident occurred.

Karen fully expected us to return to the house as soon as we were finished with the chores. However, much to her chagrin, my father and I decided to go into town to pick up some supplies without stopping by the house. To this day my wife does not recall how she finally resolved the situation with our son in the corner, but she does remember it as a very uncomfortable event.

Relater parents are often judged as being weak or ineffective because they tend to avoid conflict or confrontation. Such was the thinking of 16-year-old Don, who became very upset with his relater dad because he apparently let doer mom have her way in everything. Finally it became more than Don could bear, and he confronted his mom by saying, "Mom, I want you to stop it! I want you to stop manipulating Dad!" Later relater dad took Don aside and explained, "Son, you just don't understand. When something is really important to me, I tell your mother, and we discuss it. But why should I have my way when it is so important to your mother that she have hers? Most things just don't matter that much to me and are not worth fussing over." In other words, relationships are usually more important to relaters than position or power.

Relater parents are really not as wimpy as they may appear.

Relater parents are really not as wimpy as they may appear. In fact, relaters can be as stubborn as the proverbial Missouri mule when they have decided that enough is enough. I remember one married couple who were having some difficulty adjusting to each other.

Doer Doris was extremely upset with Relater Ron because he never seemed to finish anything he started. "In fact," she lamented, "most of the time he doesn't even start. He's about as useful as a dead battery on a cold January morning." Pausing briefly, she continued, "I asked him to fix the engine in my car a year ago, and it still isn't fixed."

I nodded my head sympathetically, and that was all the encouragement she needed.

"Oh, he pulled it out of the car, all right—after I complained to him about it for six months. But it's been out for more than a year, and he still hasn't fixed it. Not that he can't, mind you! He's a mechanic and works with cars every day. He's just doing this to spite me."

"Doing what?" I inquired.

"Leaving it on the front porch!" she shouted. "He pulled out that stupid engine and plopped it right in front of the door on our front porch. Said he wanted it under cover so he could work on it. We walk around it every morning when we go to work and every night when we get home. Don't you think that's just to spite me?"

As she told her tale of woe, I thought I noticed a slight smile at the corner of Relater Ron's mouth. But there was more.

"Furthermore," she continued, "he was always talking about building a workshop. So I encouraged him to build one. Finally, after many months of encouraging—"

"Nagging is more like it," interrupted Relater Ron.

"No, I mean encouraging," she protested. "After lots of encouraging he finally poured the foundation. But guess who finally had to build the workshop? I did!"

I looked at Relater Ron with questioning eyes.

"The truth of the matter is, I never really wanted to build a workshop," he began. "It was just sort of a dream that I could retreat to and feel comfortable with. But she made life miserable for me until I agreed to get started on the project. Because I didn't care how long it actually took to build it, she ended up finishing it off. I figured if that made her happy, so be it."

Nothing was really resolved at that session, and Doer Doris remained extremely upset with Relater Ron. I asked her why she didn't contact someone else to pick up her engine and repair it. "Because he's a mechanic and knows full well how to fix it!" she replied firmly.

Obviously, Relater Ron was not about to repair the engine. In fact, he secretly enjoyed seeing it on the front porch as a daily reminder that he would be pushed only so far.

Doer Doris also grew tired of Relater Ron's sloppy habits in the house and decided to do something dramatic to get his attention. She divided each room in half with masking tape. One half she assigned to him, and the other half was her responsibility. Even the kitchen was divided in half, beginning at the double sink. His dishes were on one side, and her dishes on the other.

I later asked her how this arrangement was working out.

"It's not!" she complained. "He won't keep his side clean."

"But I thought the whole idea was to let him do whatever he wanted with his side," I persisted, somewhat amused but trying to keep a straight face.

Relater parents sometimes serve as dumpsters for their adolescent children's guilt and problems.

"Not really," she confessed. "I actually wanted him to learn to clean up after himself, and I thought this would teach him a lesson. But there's no way I can leave half of every room a mess when people come to visit. What would they think of me?"

Perhaps you have experienced similar conflict in your own home. Even though dividing the house was somewhat unusual, the conflict between doers and relaters is not. Often relaters will amble off to the living room, slouch down on the couch, and turn on the television, rather than face the confronting anger of doers.

It is important to understand that relaters need gentle motivation rather than constant nagging.

Relater parents sometimes serve as dumpsters for their adolescent children's guilt and problems. Because relater parents will accept the role of dumpster rather than encounter confrontation, teens may not be forced to face the consequences of their actions.

♦ ♦ ♦

It has been said that among those things that are so simple that even a child can operate them are parents! The task of parents is to raise teens to maturity and not be manipulated by them. Most parents are not experts at raising children. Some feel that that distinction is reserved for grandparents! Actually, most parents mature right along with their children. Just when their children are going through their teen years, many parents are experiencing an unsettling midlife crisis. Maturity comes to both in the process.

Parents are often under considerable stress and frustration. The expectations of their friends, church family, employer, relatives, children, spouse, and even their own dreams and standards, create tension that is often difficult to define or understand. In addition, parents must contend with their own inherited strengths and weaknesses.

By learning to understand themselves, parents can learn to appreciate or at least accept the actions of their teenagers.

By learning to understand themselves, parents can learn to appreciate or at least accept the actions of their teenagers. Teens do not fit neatly into a single temperament mold any more than parents do. We humans are far too complex for such a simplistic analysis. However, an understanding of basic temperament characteristics will not only give parents insight into their own actions, but will greatly aid them in understanding their teenage children.

God made each one of us different so that we can function in our own role. He made some of us *feet*—to move, to administer, to accomplish—like the *doers*. He made some of us *minds*—to think deeply, to feel, to write—like the *thinkers*. He made some of us *hands*—to serve, to smooth, to soothe—like the *relaters*. He made some of us to be *mouths*—to talk, to teach, to encourage—like the *sellers* (paraphrased from Owen Allen, *Personality Power the Specific Action Way: A Complete Course in Management Styles*, p. 186).

Every child of God brings valuable dimension to the body of Christ. In order for the body to function properly, it needs a multitude of temperament blends, the unique blends each person has been given. As parents, try looking at your teens through Christ's eyes. Earnestly focus on their strengths and good qualities, rather than complaining about their faults. Determine to bring out the best in them by constantly complimenting them on their strengths. If that sounds like too big a task for a parent, then claim this promise from God's Word: "I can do everything God asks me to with the help of Christ who gives me the strength and power" (Phil. 4:13, TLB).

CHAPTER 4

Why Can't We Be Friends?

A teenage girl remarked, "You can't be friends with your mom. My girlfriends tell me they've tried it, and it's just a waste of time. So I don't even try."

Is this true? Is it impossible for teenagers to be friends with their parents? Perhaps. However, it appears that at least some parents and teens make it work. How do they do it?

One of the first things parents must consider is whether or not they really *want* to be friends with their adolescent children. Some parents do not want to make the transition from parent to friend. Other parents are so insecure in their own world that they find it difficult to venture into the teen world. Still others, like the girl above, think it is a waste of time and perhaps even contrary to human nature.

Parents should consider friendship with their teenagers a very serious decision that should not be taken lightly. If they decide not to become friends with their teenage offspring, it will have a lasting effect upon that relationship when they become adults. In fact, it could impact their relationship permanently.

I remember struggling with this dilemma as the father of a

teenage son. How could I make the transition from father to friend? What could I do that would make him like me as a friend rather than just respect me as a father?

Our journey was rocky at first, but I am thankful that our son was so flexible and forgiving. Looking back, I realize that I made many blunders, but neither of us gave up, and now as a young adult, he is my best male friend. How did we do it? Mainly by trial and error.

In this chapter I will reveal some of the trials and many of the errors, so that hopefully you can avoid some of my mistakes.

Friendship is everything. In the home there is really nothing stronger than friendship. If you genuinely like others, it is much easier to overlook their faults and focus on their gifts. Scripture affirms that friendship is often more powerful than blood relations. "But there is a friend who sticks closer than a brother" (Prov. 18:24, NIV). Friendship is everything in the home. It is not enough to have authority and obedience. There must also be friendship and respect.

> **In the home there is really nothing stronger than friendship.**

Sometimes friendships break down because parents must assume the role of authority. If rules in your home are more important than the family they are meant to protect, then surely friendship will be bound by a slender thread. Friendship is like marriage in that it springs from commitment to each other. Sometimes you feel good about your marriage and sometimes you feel bad, but if you are committed to your spouse, you work through the bad times. Likewise with friendship. There are ups and downs in every friendship, but these only make the bond stronger if commitment is the bond that holds people together.

Friends listen. Parents often ask me how to *make* their teenagers talk. My first response is "Simply listen." There is no substitute for listening to your teenage young people. Often we want our teens to listen to *us*, but we fail to offer *them* the same courtesy. If your work is more important than listening to your teens give a detailed description of what happened to them today, then probably you are not a very good friend.

Some parents listen only long enough to gather evidence for the next inquisition. That type of listening soon encourages your teenagers to be silent in your presence. There is so much to learn from teenage children if we will only listen and try to understand. Active listening can be difficult and is sometimes tiring, but it is always rewarding. Learn to bite your tongue if necessary to keep from interrupting your teens when they are speaking. Wait until they are finished talking, pause thoughtfully as you digest what has been said, then offer a positive comment indicating that you understand. If you do not understand, ask what they meant and try again. Encourage your teens to talk through their fears and frustrations without your putting them down or making them feel inferior.

I have heard many parents lament their parenting techniques with their teenagers, but I have not heard one parent express regret for listening.

Our son and I went through a difficult period during his teen years when I was trying to make the transition from father to friend. It wasn't easy and didn't happen overnight. However, we did manage to maintain a close enough friendship so that as he entered adulthood he felt free to talk and knew that I would listen. As I look back at his early teen years, I wish I had listened more and dictated less. I have heard many parents lament their parenting techniques with their teenagers, but I have not heard one parent express regret for listening.

When your teens start to talk with you, be quiet and listen. Do not interrupt. Every time you interrupt, it puts more distance between you. Be sympathetic, even if it kills you. Only when you quietly listen to the whole story can you find out what your teens are looking for. If it is reassurance, give it; if it is comfort, offer it; if it is guidance, carefully work it through. Do not respond with a lecture or set up new rules. If you feel you absolutely must set up new rules, do it a day or so later, calmly and with input from your teenagers.

Friends are confidants. How can teens trust their parents as friends if the parents betray their shared secrets with the world or belittle their struggles during the teen years? Teenagers must know that they are loved no matter what they do or say. Parents must learn to show unconditional love that knows no boundaries. That doesn't mean parents should not enforce household rules. True friends do not allow those they love to destroy themselves. Neither do parents allow the teens they love to self-destruct.

However, teenage children must feel confident that their parents will not use against them information that they have shared in confidence. If teens fear their parents' reactions to an admission that they tried alcohol, to whom will these teens turn as a confidant?

> **Teenagers must know that they are loved no matter what they do or say. Parents must learn to show unconditional love that knows no boundaries.**

It would be much better if the parents would listen to the entire story and then carefully draw out from their teen children any lessons they had learned from the incident. Yelling and screaming by irate parents do not foster friendship.

Friends share common interests. If parents truly wish to be friends with their teens, they must share common interests. I know one mother who listens to her teenager's compact disks so she can become familiar with the singing groups and words of their songs. She and her teen are now comfortable enough with each other's music that they can talk about it without putting each other down.

In the process, she tells me, she has developed a genuine appreciation for some of her daughter's favorite groups.

Our son, Mitch, and I have gone through an interesting transition with music. I am a child of the fifties and enjoy hearing the songs from my youth. He is a child of the seventies and finds himself stuck in the same mode with songs from that era. We talk and laugh about this and try to find songs that the other will appreciate. In the process, he has introduced me to several groups that I truly appreciate.

Mitch and I both enjoy various sports activities and keep current by sharing with each other. We are both ardent football fans and even share interest in some of the same teams. Although he is a baseball fan and I am more of a basketball fanatic, we still share with each other about our favorite sports. We are both active racing fans and faithfully follow the NASCAR circuit. We each have our favorite drivers and cannot wait to rub it in when our driver wins and the other driver loses! Friends have common interests and enjoy sharing about those interests with each other.

Some parents speak about quality time as though 30 minutes of concentrated effort could make up for a week of neglect.

Friends do things together. There is no substitute for time spent in developing a friendship. Some parents speak about quality time as though 30 minutes of concentrated effort could make up for a week of neglect. It just doesn't happen that way. There is no substitute for quantity, regardless of its quality.

When our son was a teen, I dedicated at least one week each year (sometimes more) to doing something together. I wanted this to be a special bonding time between us. We planned a different event each year. We spent a great deal of time together planning the event throughout the year. Our first week together was a bicycle trip that included camping out in a pup tent. The following year we went backpacking on the Baker Trail in the mountains of Pennsylvania. The following year we combined backpacking in the Smokies and a trip in our pop-top van. Each year we became closer friends as we planned and enjoyed these outings together.

During our son's junior year in high school, he attended a boarding academy in Wisconsin, and we lived in Seattle, Washington. It was difficult to spend time together when we were so far apart, so we made our summers extra-special. One summer we worked on his project car, a 1956 Chevy Nomad, and brought it to completion. Since we both share a common interest in automobiles, this has become a bonding point in our friendship throughout the years.

A few years ago I asked Mitch what memories stood out for him in his early teen years. Without hesitating he replied, "All those things we did together as father and son, just the two of us." His words brought tears to my eyes as I realized there really is no substitute for extended time together.

> **Teenagers lie mainly because their parents encourage them to.**

Friends are truthful. Teenagers lie mainly because their parents encourage them to. No, not with overt actions, but with subtle, unconscious ways. For example, Mitch had a good school friend whom he liked a lot. I was against him being friends with that boy because his family had a bad reputation (his brother was on drugs), and I just didn't want that kind of influence in Mitch's life. I did not take the time to get to know Mitch's friend; I just laid down the law. As a result, Mitch did not tell me when he was seeing his friend, and sometimes he would say he was going to see someone else even though he was going to his friend's house.

Why? Teens lie for a number of reasons. Sometimes because they fear being wrong. Sometimes they do not like the scene that will follow if they tell the truth. Sometimes they wish to avoid or at least postpone punishment. These are all the result of poor parenting techniques. Lying is a family affair. Families characterized by rigid boundaries, assigned high expectations, and lack of listening skills can expect lying to occur often.

Teens watch closely to see how their parents behave when it comes to "little white lies." The telephone rings and as the teen reaches for the receiver Dad says, "If it's for me, say I'm not here." A teenage daughter asks her mother to go shopping with her, and Mom replies, "I can't. I'm too tired." Then she spends the rest of the day cleaning the house. It's easy to see how lying becomes a family affair and how teens pick up on it at an early age.

The best way to discourage young persons from lying is to make it easy for them to tell the truth. Listen carefully when they speak. Spend time together. Make certain you always tell the truth. Let your teens know that lying is never OK. Point out that if they always tell the truth, they will never have to feel guilty or try to remember their lies so they can cover them up with more lies.

After forgiving an offense, urge your teenagers to be honest with you in the future and pledge your support in their time of need or understanding.

Learn to forgive your teens and teach them to claim this Bible promise: "If we confess our sins, he is faithful and just, and will forgive our sins and cleanse us from all unrighteousness" (1 John 1:9, RSV).

We all make mistakes and need forgiveness. After forgiving an offense, urge your teenagers to be honest with you in the future and pledge your support in their time of need or understanding. Often teens are trying to communicate something else with the lie. It is important for parents to figure out the message behind the lie. For example, a teen fabricates a story about doing well in sports when he didn't even make the team. He might really be saying "I want you to accept me just the way I am. But I'm afraid you will accept me only if I excel in sports or some other field."

Friends love each other. Sometimes it is difficult for parents to show love in a manner acceptable to adolescents. If you are stuck with hugging or whispering "I love you" as your only means of communicating love, let me suggest some alternatives that might get your creative juices flowing.

- On the day of a big test or important event in school, stick an encouraging note inside your teen's notebook.
- Plan a surprise "You're Great!" pizza party for your teen at her favorite pizza parlor. Invite all her favorite friends to meet you there and keep it a secret. Everyone will love it.
- Buy an uplifting card and tape it to the bathroom mirror after your teen goes to bed. It will be the first thing seen in the morning.
- Surprise your teen with the keys to the car on a night when he doesn't expect it.
- Buy a small item your teen enjoys, such as a favorite candy bar, and leave it with a note saying, "I'm proud of you!"
- Slip your teen a couple of dollars to treat her friends to frozen yogurt or a soft drink.
- Buy a poster that says "Hang in There" or "You're Special!" and hang it in your teen's room before he gets home.
- Subscribe to a magazine that focuses on your teen's favorite sport or hobby.
- Invite your teen's best friend over for dinner without telling your teen ahead of time.
- If you work outside the home during the day and your teen usually gets the mail, send a card to your teenager.
- Fill up the gas tank, and give your teen a certificate for free use of 10 gallons of gas.

> **Sometimes it is difficult for parents to show love in a manner acceptable to adolescents.**

Now that you are thinking of ways to show your love to your teenage children, remember to constantly share with them that God not only loves them but is also their friend.

"No longer do I call you servants, for the servant does not know what his master is doing; but I have called you friends, for all that I have heard from my Father I have made known to you" (John 15:15, RSV). "A friend loves at all times" (Prov. 17:17, RSV).

Encourage your adolescent children to make Jesus their best friend, and assure them that you will be happy to be a little lower on the list!

ADVICE FROM PARENTS WHO MADE IT WORK

Gary and Phyllis Charles, parents of Steven, 22; Jennifer, 15; Adam, 13—"We made a conscious effort with our kids to build a relation of trust and always be there for them. We communicate through actions. We read facial expressions and body language. When we see danger signs, then by asking a gentle question or two we can bring it out in the open and talk about it."

Share with them that God is their friend.

Cheryle and Walter Allen, parents of Elizabeth, 15—"It takes Elizabeth an hour to get around to what's really on her mind. First, she wants to find out if we're really concerned about her or just making conversation. It takes patience to listen without offering advice. Sometimes Elizabeth just wants a little of our time; this makes her feel special and loved."

Gerald and Sandy Brooks, parents of Gene, 21, and Chris, 16—"We may have finally discovered the secret of loosening Chris's lips; he talks more when he's riding in the car. Another thing is that he recently got a weekend job. He's learning to smile and talk to customers whether he's comfortable with it or not."

Gary and Linda Bradley, parents of Kristin, 17; Jason, 15; Matt and Ben, 13 (twins)—"Prayer can soften hearts and open minds, and that makes both parent and teen able to listen more effectively to one another."

Cindy Ryan, single parent of Katrina, 15—"God loves Katrina more than I do. He will redeem my mistakes. I let her know that I'm on her side. Once when she was hurt by something that happened at school, she directed her anger at me. I wanted to feel sorry for myself, but the Lord said, 'Don't forget, you're on her side.' As long as I keep telling her who she is in God, the enemy can't fill her head full of lies."

Dick Davis, father of Marc, 18, and Matt, 15—"We involve ourselves in our kids' interests. Matt wants to be a doctor, so I read a lot of medical books and publications. Marc and I are building a house together."

Kelvin and Robina Burton, parents of Amy, 14, and Sara, 13—"We have family prayer times that allow the kids to pray for each other. We also have praise times to thank God for providing. We like to lead by example. If we're teaching them something, we use examples from our own experiences."

We like to lead by example. If we're teaching them something, we use examples from our own experiences.

Nancy and Anthony Roden, parents of Bud, 18 (Nancy's son by a previous marriage); Jenn, 4; John, 3—"Bud is closer to Anthony than he is to his natural father. I think it's because Bud considers Anthony nonthreatening; no matter what he tells him. He responds to him as a friend (they play golf together) instead of a stepfather."

Deyon Stephens, mother of Luke, 19, and John Paul, 16—"We made family mealtimes a requirement; it allows for meaningful communication. My husband likes to plan outings like swimming, fishing, or going to a theme park." (From *Parents & Teens*, July/August 1992, pp. 12, 13.)

PT-3

CHAPTER 5

Teaching Your Teens About Relationships

It has been said that youth is that period between childhood and middle age during which the sexes talk to each other at parties.

Whether or not this is true, teenagers do spend a lot of time talking to members of the opposite sex. The teen years are a time for building relationships with both sexes—but especially with members of the opposite sex. It is a time when each relationship seems to be the one that romance novels are written about. It is a time when infatuation occurs on a regular basis. The teen years are a time when children are transformed into adults.

During this time of uncertainty, teenage children must deal with peer pressure, insecurity, physical changes, emotional upheaval, infatuation, sexual attraction, and romance. Such pressures, along with a lack of previous experience, often cause teenagers to rush into relationships that they later regret for the rest of their lives.

One of my favorite *Peanuts* cartoons is from many years ago, when Sally was still a toddler. One day she was crawling along the floor while Linus and Lucy watched her progress with obvious interest.

Linus asked, "How long do you think it will be before Sally starts to walk?"

Lucy shot back, "Good grief! What's the hurry? Let her crawl around for a while! Don't rush her! She's got all the time in the world. Once you stand up and start to walk, you're committed for life."

If you take nothing else with you from this book, I hope it is this: Don't let your teens be in a hurry to establish permanent relationships or to make lifelong commitments. They have the rest of their lives. Teach them how to crawl in a relationship before they try to run. Finding the *right* relationship takes time, effort, practice, and patience. One way that parents can guide their teenage youngsters in this area is to talk with them about the wrong reasons for having a relationship.

Infatuation—If they feel they cannot live without a certain individual, they probably should look elsewhere before it is too late. Often, inexperienced teens assume that such a strong feeling for another person must be love, when in reality it is infatuation. Given enough time it will wear off and leave them with the reality of the relationship. If it is immature or premature, the relationship may not have the necessary ingredients to endure.

> **Don't let your teens be in a hurry to establish permanent relationships or to make lifelong commitments.**

Sexual Attraction—Whenever your teens feel "so good" in the physical presence of another, be careful. That is usually sexual attraction trying to scramble their brains. Whenever they let their hormones and sex organs determine a relationship, it is a sign that they are going too fast. Encourage them to slow down! Back off! Maybe even break up (if your relationship with your teen is strong enough to support that statement). Such a strong physical attraction is another symptom of an immature or premature relationship.

Romantic Attraction—"But she understands me completely!"

"No matter what I say he finds it interesting." "Her whole world is focused on my happiness." "He never tires of listening to me." "She thinks I'm witty and intelligent, and she always says the right words to make me feel important." While these are all positive qualities in a relationship, it takes time to determine whether or not they are lasting qualities. Many times these qualities disappear after a few weeks or months. This romantic attraction may actually blind your teens to the real foundation in a permanent relationship . . . *love!*

Why do relationships fail when everything seems so right? There are many reasons for failure in today's mobile, noncommitted, selfish society. Today's dating couples no longer need parental approval for dating, mating, and hating, which is the usual order of events in an immature relationship. Our society has relaxed the rules and in many cases even forgotten them. Broken engagements are no longer the source of scandal or neighborhood gossip. How can they be when one out of every two marriages in the past decade has ended in divorce? Commitment seems to be a forgotten word in today's relationship vocabulary.

Commitment seems to be a forgotten word in today's relationship vocabulary.

When I think of commitment, I think of my father. For him, his word was as good as a contract, and he never went back on it. I can remember him going to the bank and borrowing money simply on his promise to repay. The banker knew my father's character and was confident that he would repay the loan. So confident, in fact, that he did not require any collateral, merely his signature. That is the type of commitment necessary for a lasting relationship. Commitment establishes confidence, confidence encourages trust, and genuine trust is the product of trial and error, which takes *time*. There is no way for teenagers to shorten the process without leaving out a valuable ingredient or necessary step. Only time will reveal whether the commitment is real and trust is justified.

Relationships also fail because society in general no longer accepts biblical principles concerning sexual morality. Many people no longer consider living together a sin. In fact, some view it as part of the maturation process. Such shortsighted views ignore the true foundation in any relationship—commitment. The Bible emphasizes the permanence of marriage by comparing it to our relationship with God.

"For this reason a man will leave his father and mother and be united to his wife, and the two will become one flesh. This is a profound mystery—but I am talking about Christ and the church" (Eph. 5:31, 32, NIV).

The choice of words here implies that God intended for both relationships to be secure and permanent. This is comforting since we certainly wouldn't want our relationship with God to be merely a temporary "live-in" arrangement. Encourage your teenagers not to settle for anything less than total, permanent commitment from their most important relationships here on earth.

> **A good rule of thumb for all teens is this: What you see *is* what you get! If you don't like what you see—get someone else.**

Another reason teen relationships fail is because they expect too much from the other person. They expect their future partner to change in order to meet *their* needs, desires, and fantasies. Yet they seldom extend that same courtesy to the other person. Working through the early stages of a relationship often requires much effort, pain, and adjustment before they resolve personality and temperament differences. A good rule of thumb for all teens is this: *What you see is what you get! If you don't like what you see—get someone else.*

If adolescents report that a relationship seems to be "too good to be true," they may be missing another vital ingredient—*honesty*. Sometimes it is painful to share the truth with someone we care for, but it is always liberating. Relationships built upon lies, half-truths, and concealed feelings will probably fail. Unfortunately, this failure often takes place after they have gone further than intended in what turns out to be just a temporary relationship.

"Love at first sight" is another cause of failed relationships. There may be infatuation at first sight, or sexual attraction at first sight, but there can never be true love at first sight. Love is built upon the basic relational ingredients of commitment, honesty, confidence, and trust. How can all these ingredients be present at first sight? Such basic ingredients for a permanent relationship are discovered only with time!

"Love at first sight" should probably be described as "lust at first sight." Your teens' whole world seems brighter; no problem is insurmountable; nothing can stand in their way; together they can conquer the world . . . at least until the glow of infatuation begins to fade. The reality of a permanent relationship is putting up with bad breath or whiskers when you don't feel [or look] too good yourself.

There are three stages in a relationship: the friendship stage, the dating stage, and the sexual stage. In that order!

Jim Talley, in *Too Close Too Soon*, suggests there are three stages in a relationship: the friendship stage, the dating stage, and the sexual stage. In that order! Most relationships should never go beyond the friendship stage; a few should advance to the dating stage; but the final stage should be reserved for a permanent relationship.

Friendship—During this stage teens become acquainted with each other on a social, recreational, spiritual, intellectual, and communicative level. It is a time for sharing. There are no sexual connotations, no lifelong commitments, just a mutual respect for one another. Probably most of their friends and acquaintances fall into this category.

Dating—If the friendship stage mutually matures, they will probably enter the dating stage. This is a time for physical intimacies that would be inappropriate if they were just friends. A physical attachment develops, and the teens seem almost inseparable. Their friends have gotten used to them turning down invitations so they can spend time with their special friend. During this stage an emotional attachment develops as well. They can't seem to live without each other. They constantly think, fantasize, and dream about these persons who have taken priority in their lives.

At this point difficulties often arise in a relationship. Males and females seem to arrive at this stage with differing agendas. The normal agenda for a male is to become physically intimate before becoming emotionally involved. Females want just the opposite: emotional commitment prior to physical intimacy. Unless both parties realize what is happening, they may make decisions or assumptions based on misconceptions concerning the relationship.

Unless both parties realize what is happening, they may make decisions or assumptions based on misconceptions concerning the relationship.

If a female believes that the desire for physical intimacy follows emotional intimacy, she may assume that the male in her life has already made an emotional commitment if he desires more intimate physical involvement. She may even assume that her partner is ready to make a permanent commitment that would result in marriage. Often the relationship ends at this point, when the male discovers the depth of the female's emotional attachment. He becomes alarmed and wants out. If sexual intimacy has already taken place, it is usually the female who suffers most from the broken relationship, since she has made an emotional attachment but the male has not.

True intimacy takes time to develop. Because males and females arrive at the various stages of a relationship at different times, this should go slowly. For her own protection the female should refrain from physical intimacies until her partner has had time to make an emotional commitment. This takes time, but will reveal the true feelings of her boyfriend. Likewise the male should refrain from initiating physical intimacies until he has made an emotional commitment. To do otherwise would be dishonest and send a false signal to his girlfriend.

True intimacy takes time to develop. Because males and females arrive at the various stages of a relationship at different times, this should go slowly.

The comic strip *Momma* offers some interesting insight into this aspect of a relationship. As you may know, Momma is always trying to straighten out her three grown children. One of the continuing themes is the proper courtship and eventual marriage of her daughter, Mary Lou. One day Momma asked Mary Lou why she wasn't married yet.

Mary Lou responded: "Nobody's proposed, Momma, although I do seem to be very popular with the boys."

Momma retorts: "Well, whatever is making you popular with the boys—STOP IT until one of them proposes."

Once both partners have arrived at the same stage of emotional commitment, they face the third stage of this kind of relationship—*sex*. God intended that sex be a lifelong stage of learning and exploration secured by the commitment of marriage vows. During this stage both parties should feel safe to reveal themselves fully and completely, in the most intimate sense, to their marriage partner. In fact, the Bible makes it quite clear that in marriage we offer ourselves completely to our partner.

"The wife's body does not belong to her alone but also to her husband. In the same way, the husband's body does not belong to him alone but also to his wife. Do not deprive each other except by mutual consent" (1 Cor. 7:4, 5, NIV).

For a relationship to go from *introduction* to the *bedroom* usually takes about 300 hours of togetherness (see Jim Talley, *Too Close Too Soon*, p. 33). For previously married individuals, the process may be somewhat faster. For those separated geographically, it may take longer. Talley found that time spent together prior to sexual activity is approximately 75 four-hour dates or 50 six-hour dates or 25 twelve-hour days together. As you can see, the more compressed the time span, the sooner sex enters into a relationship.

Romance and infatuation are both addictive and are difficult for teenagers to set aside once they have gotten involved with them. The couple want to spend more and more time together, which rapidly uses up the 300-hour cushion available at the beginning of their relationship. Moreover, the law of diminishing returns soon sets in, and the couple find it necessary to resort to more and more intimate behavior in order to maintain the same level of excitement. At this point it is time for them to stop and think. It's quite possible that they might make the mistake of entering a sexual relationship simply because they are addicted to certain feelings.

For a relationship to go from *introduction* to the *bedroom* usually takes about 300 hours of togetherness.

So how can they control a relationship in order to preserve the sexual stage for marriage? Talley recommends that they follow the AAA method of control, which involves carefully monitoring attitude, activities, and accumulated time together!

Attitude—Many teens fall into premature sexual relationships because of low self-esteem. Their negative image of themselves can push them into an unhealthy relationship or premature marriage in order to find affirmation.

Their attitude should be one of *respect*: respect for the One who created them, respect for themselves, and respect for their partner in the relationship. If such respect is present, you can acknowledge their natural sexual desires for each other, but their respect for God, themselves, and their partner will prevent premarital (and premature) sex. Sexual desires should be acknowledged during dating, but fulfillment of those desires should wait until they have established a permanent marriage relationship.

"It is God's will that you should be sanctified; that you should avoid sexual immorality; that each of you should learn to control his own body in a way that is holy and honorable, not in passionate lust like the heathen, who do not know God; and that in this matter no one should wrong his brother or take advantage of him. The Lord will punish men for all such sins, as we have already told you and warned you. For God did not call us to be impure, but to live a holy life. Therefore, he who rejects this instruction does not reject man but God, who gives his Holy Spirit" (1 Thess. 4:3-8, NIV).

> **Many teens fall into premature sexual relationships because of low self-esteem.**

Another drawback of engaging in premarital sex is that it may be a stumbling block for the partner who may be acting contrary to his or her own conscience in order to fulfill the other person's desires. Forcing a partner to choose between God and self may even plant the seeds that will ultimately destroy the relationship. Or, worse yet, a person may cause the partner to dissolve the relationship with God.

Activities—Carefully monitor how teens spend their time together. A walk in a crowded park with friends is preferable to a walk in a secluded woods alone. Working on projects together is far better than making out in a parked car. Teach them how to have fun together, not just turn each other on.

By all means encourage them to spend time discussing their spiritual lives together. What do they want to accomplish for God? What do they see as God's purpose for their life? Where do they see God leading in this relationship? What is their commitment to God? What measure of spiritual commitment do they expect from a future partner? Teach them to choose topics of conversation that will focus their thoughts on their partner's dreams and aspirations rather than upon their sexual desires. Talking about spiritual things and praying together will help them resist sexual temptation.

One of the best ways for teens to overcome their sexual urges, without sex, is through rigorous physical activity. Playing a few fast sets of tennis is a lot safer in a 300-hour relationship than necking behind the bleachers.

Accumulated Time Together— Don't forget about the 300-hour average from introduction to sexual encounter. Therefore, limit the time they spend *alone* together. For example, if they dated one day a week for three hours, it would take 1.5 years to reach 300 hours. However, if they increased their dating frequency from once a week to every night, it would take only 2.5 months to reach the same level. If they dated every night plus weekends, they would arrive at the 300-hour level in six weeks. Monitoring time spent together will help them avoid premature decisions made in a moment of passion.

Limit the time they spend *alone* together.

Encourage your teenage young people to take time for themselves and spend time doing things alone. In addition, they should
- devote special time to their family.
- spend time with God and get to know Him better.
- take time to be with other friends they have been neglecting since meeting their special friend.

- pour themselves into their studies during the week and devote one or two nights to recreation and exercise outside the relationship.
- attend to their regular daily responsibilities that are often neglected during the dating stage.

Talley recommends that after they have spent 100 hours in dating, a couple who are "serious" about each other should seek counseling from a class, a professional counselor, or a teacher. It is also time to discuss their future together as a couple and make a mutual commitment to refrain from sexual intimacies unless they marry. This discussion will bring all aspects of their relationship into the light of day. It will allow them to speak openly and honestly about what each one of them wants from a permanent relationship. Such discussions may reveal flaws in their relationship and cause them to rethink their commitment. It is better to discover a mismatch now than after the marriage ceremony.

Talley recommends that after they have spent 100 hours in dating, a couple who are "serious" about each other should seek counseling.

Mel Lazarus, in *Momma*, features Mary Lou cuddling on the front porch with her boyfriend, and he is whispering sweet nothings in her ear. Momma is trying to eavesdrop from the window, but can't hear what's going on. When Mary Lou finally comes back into the house, Momma asks, "Mary Lou, what did he whisper to you?"

Mary Lou replies, "Ah, just love stuff, Momma."

Momma replies, "Decent 'love stuff' can be spoken freely, out loud. . . . Decent 'love stuff' can be shouted from the rooftops." Finally her voice reaches a resounding crescendo as she shouts, "Decent 'love stuff' can be embroidered on samplers!"

Talley also recommends some helpful hints to help teens control the fires of passion while dating in a serious relationship. They can

1. agree to limit their time alone together. It is much easier when both agree to such limits.

2. plan their dates in advance rather than doing whatever "feels good" at the moment.

3. spend much of their dating time actively involved in school projects, sports, or other nonintimate activities.

4. refrain from all behaviors that sexually arouse their partner. To do so deliberately is manipulative and indicates an immature attitude toward a permanent relationship.

5. avoid erotic literature, movies, or pictures.

6. refrain from participating in an obviously dangerous situation, such as a candlelight dinner, intimate mood music when alone, or even necking in the corner of the porch.

7. be open and honest with each other about behavior and situations that turn them on or make it difficult for them to resist sexual intimacies.

> "Trust in the Lord and do good; dwell in the land and enjoy safe pasture."

8. claim this promise: "Trust in the Lord and do good; dwell in the land and enjoy safe pasture. Delight yourself in the Lord and he will give you the desires of your heart" (Ps. 37:3, 4, NIV).

Someone wrote to the editor of a Christian magazine to ask how a couple could be assured of having a happy and harmonious marriage. The editor answered with a story about two children who had been told to practice a piano duet until it was perfect. A few minutes later one of the children was found playing in the backyard sandbox. His mother scolded him for leaving the piano, but he protested, "But Mom, I finished first!"

No relationship will survive if one person leaves before the duet is perfected. Irreversible damage is done when two individuals rush into a supposedly permanent duet and it turns out to be a heartbroken solo.

Norman Wright, in *Guidebook to Dating* (pp. 145, 146), offers the following insights into the differences between *love* and *sex* in a relationship:

Love is a process; you must go through it in order to understand it. *Sex* is a performance; you have some idea of what it is like prior to going through it.

Love is a learned operation; you must learn what to do through first having been loved and cared for by someone else. *Sex* is known naturally; you know instinctively what to do.

Love requires constant attention. *Sex* is easily available and requires little effort.

Love is experienced by slow growth and takes time to develop and evolve. *Sex* develops quickly and needs only an urge to develop.

No relationship will survive if one person leaves before the duet is perfected.

Love is deepened by creative thinking. *Sex* is controlled through feelings or by responding to stimuli.

Love is many small behavioral changes that bring about good feelings. *Sex* is one big feeling brought about by one big behavior.

Love is an act of the will with or without good feelings. In fact, sometimes love doesn't "feel like it," but does it anyway. *Sex* is also an act of will, but you feel like doing it.

Love involves respect of the other person in order for it to develop. *Sex* does not require the respect of the person.

Love is lots of warm fuzzies and genuine laughter. *Sex* is an intense struggle with little or no laughter.

Love requires knowing how to interact, to talk, to develop interesting conversations thoughtfully. *Sex* requires little or no talking and virtually nothing in common except an urge.

Love develops in depth to sustain the relationship and involves much effort, out of which real happiness is eventually found. *Sex* promises a permanent relationship that seldom happens. Sex cannot sustain a relationship, but merely promises an illusion.

Actually, reserving sex for marriage makes teenagers *free!* Free from an unwanted pregnancy or a forced marriage. Free from the complications and uncertainty of birth control. Free from sexually transmitted diseases—including AIDS. Free from early sterilization caused by a sexually transmitted disease or an abortion. Free from having to make the decision on whether or not to have an abortion. Free from the guilt of disobeying God or manipulating the partner. Free from the fear of conceiving a child they are not ready to support. Forgetting about the consequences in the passion of a moment may lead to a lifetime of regret.

By learning (and practicing) self-control, they will be better marriage partners when the time is right. How reassuring it would be to know that they could trust their partner not to succumb to sexual temptations outside the marriage relationship. After all, if persons could not practice self-control before marriage, how could there be total trust in them after marriage? Also, by practicing self-control they will have the pleasure of sharing the most intimate of all experiences with only *one* person. The knowledge of sharing a completely unique experience never shared with another person will bring a special excitement and adventure into their marriage as they explore the third stage of their relationship.

Reserving sex for marriage makes teenagers free!

The following letters were written by parents to their teenage son and daughter. Read them together with your teens and discuss them.

Dear Wade [age 14]:

Sometimes I have to search for the right words when we are together, so I have decided to write this letter to you. You are the physical size of a man now, taller than I am, and I'm proud of every inch of you. You are also growing and gaining experience intellectually. You have always been a clear, perceptive thinker, particularly about knowing yourself and knowing what your own needs are.

You will be playing football this fall at school. I'm sure that you know what the locker room conversation is about with a group of teenage boys. It's OK to know who you are, to take pride in yourself, and to make your own decisions about what to say and what to laugh at.

You have a strong body and a good brain. Take care of them both. Recognize that you also have emotional needs to be met. You are becoming a sexual person, and that is normal and wonderful at the same time. **It is OK and normal to have sexual feelings for a girl, and it's OK and normal not to do anything about those feelings.** These are decisions that only you can make.

Remember, you are important to me, and I love you very much.
Dad

Dear J.J. [age 17]:

You are a beautiful, sexy-looking girl. Your emerging sexuality adds a new aspect to your life. You still have areas in which you need and want to be dependent. It's important for you to know who you are and where you are in your own sexual development. You can feel your sexual feelings without doing anything about them. Take the time you need to explore your sexuality. You will find new ways of relating to girls, to women, to your brothers, to boys, to men, and especially to your father. You do not have to have sexual intercourse because all the kids are doing it, because a national survey says that half the girls your age have, or because someone pressures you to do it. That is your decision. You can decide. Make it a responsible one for yourself and for others. I look forward to your separation, and I look forward to your return to our family as an equal adult. I will enjoy that very much. My heart is full of love for you. I trust you to become the strong, capable, full, wonderful woman that I see emerging now.

Love, Mom

CHAPTER 6

Teaching Your Teens About Sex

As a society we worship at the altar of sex. It's the payoff. Not everyone can have the goodies, the power, the money, but everyone can have sex and it will be wonderful" (Joanne Rocco Bruno, Planned Parenthood of Eastern Pennsylvania, *Global Perspectives on Adolescent Pregnancy*, p. 10).

Chances are much of what your own parents taught you about sex was inaccurate or at least misleading. So how do you go about teaching your teens about sex and its proper place in the life of Christians?

Current statistics indicate that teenage pregnancies cost our nation more than $16 billion a year and result in a tremendous dropout rate in schools. In fact, 70 percent of teenage mothers under the age of 15 drop out of school, creating a burden upon themselves, their families, and society.

Why are so many teenage girls becoming pregnant during this period of "sexual enlightenment"? Perhaps it is because sex seldom takes its proper place in modern relationships. More often than not, it is the *only* reason for the relationship. In Washington, D.C., the average teenager defines a long-term relationship as one that lasts from three weeks to three months (see *Psychology Today*, January/February 1989, p. 10). During that brief period of time sex is expected to play an important role. If it does not, a couple runs the risk of ridicule and peer pressure.

Everything is happening so fast today. How can we make sense of it all? Dr. Charles Wittschiebe used an interesting simile to illustrate the difficulty of controlling sex in a relationship. "Sex is like a horse, a spirited horse," he wrote. "You don't want him to throw you, but you don't want to lock him in the barn or drug him. He's there to be ridden, controlled, and enjoyed. Abusing him, misusing him, losing control, does away with the fun of having him" (*Teens and Love and Sex*, p. 82).

How do you teach your adolescent children to control that spirited steed called sex?

In his book *Too Close Too Soon*, Jim Talley offers the following insights: "Infatuation, sexual attraction, and romantic attachment make people feel so good in the presence of the object of those emotions that the experience is labeled 'true love' and expected to last forever. Yet true love is so much more than good feelings. It is the choice to invest in the life of a beloved, not only when it feels good but also when it doesn't" (pp. 14, 15).

> **One *falls* into infatuation, but one *grows* into love.**

Perhaps the first lesson about sex you might want to share with your teens is the difference between *infatuation* and *love*. You can appear wise beyond your years with this simple explanation: One *falls* into infatuation, but one *grows* into love. Most infatuation is a relatively short-term attraction. In a relationship of only three weeks to six months, it's obvious that what is felt isn't love. What fuels a relationship at that point is either infatuation or lust or both. It takes time for love to develop and mature to the point where it is recognizable. Infatuation often meets an emotional need such as a low self-image or recovery from a broken relationship.

When the relationship is based on infatuation, those involved think of nothing else. Their thought processes are continually interrupted by fantasies. Infatuation, mistaken for love, is the cause of many pregnancies, broken relationships, and even family problems.

Love grows and matures slowly over a period of months and years. It is certainly true that infatuation can grow into love, but too often it merely draws two people together in a premature relationship that they believe to be love. Too often, by the time they realize it isn't love, they are married or expecting a child or both! Unfortunately, sex usually rears its demanding head during the infatuation stage, when teenagers are least able to deal with it.

You might even admit how this insight has given you a different perspective about your own dating days. Tell them how you coped (or failed to cope) with sexual urges. Tell them that even though they do not fully understand this spirited steed called sex, you want them to learn how to control it before it runs away with them.

Infatuation, mistaken for love, is the cause of many pregnancies, broken relationships, and even family problems.

Dr. Wittschiebe changed metaphors to make another powerful point concerning sex in a relationship. "Biological attraction should furnish the electricity for the relationship, but it should not be allowed to become so overpowering that it short-circuits the entire relationship" (*Teens and Love and Sex*, p. 37).

One way to approach the subject of sex and infatuation would be to remind your teens that puberty is a time of powerful changes and relate to them how you felt at their age. Most parents have several vivid recollections permanently engraved in their minds. At first you may not feel comfortable talking with your teenage children about your own fears and sexual misinformation during your teen years, but forge ahead anyway.

Infatuation is especially deceptive for teens, since many young people feel insecure and may suffer from low self-esteem. The emotional high of infatuation provides a temporary lift for their self-image. But remember that although the infatuation balloon ascends rapidly, it often comes crashing down when punctured by the tack of reality. Infatuation can become so overpowering that those suffering from it may lose interest in their friends, church, or even God.

In fact, one way to determine whether or not a relationship is the result of infatuation is to ask your teens this question: "Does this relationship consume most of your thought processes and time?" If it does, it is probably infatuation rather than love. Love is not demanding or possessive. Love allows your teens to focus on a wide variety of interests without detracting from the relationship. In one of your honest moments, confess that you had a number of early relationships that began with infatuation. Then explain how one or more of them grew into love. If you are divorced or are having current difficulties in your marriage, you may want to think through your own problems before discussing love with your teenage young people.

> **Although the infatuation balloon ascends rapidly, it often comes crashing down when punctured by the tack of reality.**

If you are a father, you might admit how worried you were in class when a sudden unexpected erection occurred just as the teacher called upon you to come to the front of the room and give an impromptu presentation. Or how your first nocturnal emission left you feeling guilty and confused about both your feelings and the stain on the bedsheets. As a father, you probably recall some of the locker room bravado that was passed off as sexual "experience" and how none of the guys you knew would admit to being a virgin (even though most of them probably were). It will make your teenage son feel more comfortable if you assure him that your generation still shares some of those same mistaken ideas concerning manhood. Then assure him that you believe manhood is made up of much more than crude jokes, bragging, and "scoring."

Mothers may be more reluctant to share early experiences, especially when they concern sexual urges or related happenings. You may be embarrassed to admit to your teenage daughter that you were not psychologically (or perhaps even physiologically) prepared for your first menstruation. Of course you will probably refer to this passage into womanhood as your "period" or that "time of the month." Your parents probably never referred to this rite of passage as menstruation, and probably not many of your daughter's friends do either.

> **Unlike the strong sex drive that seems to appear in the male almost overnight, the female sex drive follows a rather gradual curve from preadolescence through the early 20s.**

Unlike the strong sex drive that seems to appear in the male almost overnight, the female sex drive follows a rather gradual curve from preadolescence through the early 20s. If you are the mother you might confess that you cannot remember a specific time when your sex drive first began to awaken. You will probably remember that it happened rather slowly and almost imperceptibly throughout a number of years. Assure your teen that she is perfectly normal since the female sex drive does awaken at a much slower pace, often starting earlier and peaking later.

Many mothers will recall pajama parties at which all the girls stayed over at a friend's house and talked about boys all night. Or perhaps you might recall how you felt when you received your first kiss or the first fumbling attempts of a boy to fondle your breasts.

Sometimes fathers and mothers discover that they are still

struggling with sex as something *dirty*. Some psychologists feel that parents picked up this mistaken concept as the result of improper toilet training.

The scenario may have gone something like this: Little Mary is busy playing with the other children and does not want to take time out to go to the bathroom. She plays too long and soon finds she has relieved herself in her clothes.

Mother walks by and notices what has happened. "What in the world are you doing?" she yells. "Now look what you have done! You're a *dirty* little girl. Shame on you!"

When you compound these words with being marched into the bathroom to get *cleaned up*, you begin to understand the association of one's sex organs with being dirty.

Or maybe it was Fearless Freddy, always willing to take a dare. Some of the children dare him to pull down his pants. Just as he accepts the dare and his pants are down around his ankles, Father walks by.

Children are often taught that the sex organs are shameful, when in fact the problem is merely one of proper social graces in a particular society.

"Freddy! Get those pants back up this instant. I can't believe what I'm seeing. What is the matter with you, anyway? Don't you know that is *dirty*?"

Children are often taught that the sex organs are shameful, when in fact the problem is merely one of proper social graces in a particular society. Actually, the sex organs are very clean. Both the penis and urethra discharge urine, which is a sterile waste product, from the human body. Both male and female sex organs are actually much cleaner than the average mouth.

Sex organs are covered not because they are dirty, but because they are *private*. Our society considers them to be our "private parts," and it is not considered good manners to display them in public. In addition, sexual sins are the result of our mind, not our sex organs. They merely do what the mind tells them to do. If we want to cover something in shame, perhaps it should be our heads, where the sexual sin originates.

Often when a parent catches a child masturbating or "playing doctor" with another child, the parent's reaction causes the children to feel guilty or dirty. The association is made at a very early age that anything associated with our sexual organs is bad or *dirty*.

As a child, you may have unwittingly interrupted your parents while they were having sex. Perhaps their startled reaction and physical position may have given you the impression that sex was dirty. It would be quite natural for children to conclude that with such moaning and physical pounding, something bad must be happening! If you also happened to catch a glimpse of pornographic pictures or magazines some kid brought to school, you may have concluded that sex was at least lewd if not downright dirty. In that context you were right. This is far from what God had in mind when He created us male and female. Sin has resulted in the exploitation of all natural acts, including sex.

If we want to cover something in shame, perhaps it should be our heads, where the sexual sin originates.

There are many Bible texts that refer to the recommended relationship between sex and marriage. Here are a few to review together with your teenage children.

"The body is not meant for sexual immorality, but for the Lord, and the Lord for the body" (1 Cor. 6:13, NIV).

"But since there is so much immorality, each man should have his own wife, and each woman her own husband" (1 Cor. 7:2, NIV).

"I am afraid that when I come again my God will humble me before you, and I will be grieved over many who have sinned earlier and have not repented of the impurity, sexual sin and debauchery in which they have indulged" (2 Cor. 12:21, NIV).

"The acts of the sinful nature are obvious: sexual immorality, impurity and debauchery" (Gal. 5:19, NIV).

"But among you there must not be even a hint of sexual immorality, or of any kind of impurity, or of greed, because these are improper for God's holy people" (Eph. 5:3, NIV).

"Put to death, therefore, whatever belongs to your earthly nature: sexual immorality, impurity, lust, evil desires and greed, which is idolatry" (Col. 3:5, NIV).

"It is God's will that you should be sanctified; that you should avoid sexual immorality; that each of you should learn to control his own body in a way that is holy, and honorable, not in passionate lust like the heathen, who do not know God" (1 Thess. 4:3-5, NIV).

> **"The acts of the sinful nature are obvious: sexual immorality, impurity and debauchery."**

These are pretty heavy texts, and they apply to adults as well as to teenagers. It may interest your teenage children to know that God has a reason for condemning extramarital sex (sex outside of marriage). Frankly, this gift from God is too precious to be wasted. Like the alabaster jar that Mary broke to anoint Jesus' feet, once broken it can never be put back together again. Teens often view sex like the forbidden tree in the Garden of Eden. It is pleasant to look at, the fruit appears exquisite, so why not pluck it and try it?

Just as the tree in the garden referred to a relationship (between God and the first couple), so sex refers to a relationship. Adam and Eve ate of the forbidden tree because they were told it possessed knowledge. Many teens engage in premarital sex for the same reason, to gain knowledge. A little knowledge can be deadly, especially in today's world. In fact, teens often gain just enough knowledge about sex to get themselves into deep and permanent trouble.

Teens who engage in premarital sex make a statement about their partner that is not very flattering. Infatuation would have your teens believe that because they "love" this person so much, it must be OK. But what if it isn't really love? What if it is temporary infatuation that might never grow into love? What if it is just plain old-fashioned selfish lust? What if you contract a venereal disease? What if you become infected with AIDS? What if a pregnancy occurs? What if you fall out of "love"? What if . . . what if . . . what if?

You see, without making a permanent, legal commitment to their partner, they are actually robbing that person of a precious gift and putting themselves in danger. Unless they are fully prepared to take all the risks and responsibilities inherent in the sex act, they are merely *using* the other person to satisfy their own personal needs. Love is a *giver*; lust is a *user* and ultimately a loser.

Love is a *giver*; lust is a *user* and ultimately a loser.

However, I am not so naive as to think that teenagers do not engage in sex. Statistics show that by the age of 13, the majority of males have engaged in sex, and by the age of 15, the same is true for the majority of females.

A study at Indiana University concluded that to tell boys not to have sex because they will feel bad about it is ludicrous, even though this is probably true for most girls (*USA Today*, Jan. 16, 1989).

Another survey found that four out of five teenage boys indicated that morality was very important to them (*Parade*, Dec. 18, 1988).

This dichotomy causes tremendous inner tension in many teens.

In his book *Teens and Love and Sex* (pp. 18-23) Dr. Charles

Wittschiebe offers some interesting reasons teens have given him for having sex outside of the marriage commitment. These are, of course, merely some of the sexual topics that you might discuss with your teenage children, but they will at least get you started.

1. *I [male] need to get some experience before marriage.*

What will this experience cost you and your wife? It means that you will miss out on sharing these special "firsts" with her. Chastity (that means reserving this gift for your eventual mate) and ignorance are not the same thing. Reading will prepare you for your wedding night. Talking to a trusted married friend or to your parents will prepare you. Sex education will prepare you. It is not necessary to practice, since you have the rest of your life to make sex perfect. As Wittschiebe says: "It's like enjoying a private garden instead of sharing a public park" (p. 18).

2. *We are already married in the sight of God.*

To become "one flesh" requires more than the sex act. Such a relationship implies a lifelong commitment made with a public declaration. There is much more to marriage than a ceremony. That only gives opportunity for a public declaration in the presence of witnesses. As one of my favorite writers puts it: Marriage is "the work of the afteryears" and a school from which, in this life, we shall never graduate (Ellen G. White, *The Adventist Home*, p. 105).

3. *Sex is the "true wedding" for those who really love each other.*

There is a valid reason our society requires certificates of marriage and some form of public expression. Such requirements force the individuals to count the cost of the commitment they are about to make. Marriage is more than sex. It is a commitment that

> **To become "one flesh" requires more than the sex act. Such a relationship implies a lifelong commitment.**

two individuals make to each other in the presence of witnesses and that is verified with legal documents.

4. We are engaged; therefore, it is all right.

Actually, long engagements can be more destructive than productive. It is one thing to be engaged long enough to get to know each other and plan a future together, but it is unwise to prolong engagement when there is a strong physical attraction.

Paul offers the following warning: "If [the unmarried] cannot control themselves, they should marry, for it is better to marry than to burn with passion" (1 Cor. 7:9, NIV).

5. Sex indicates the true depth of our love for each other.

This particular statement is usually offered by the male. It represents the most selfish form of love. "If you love me, you will _____." Such reasoning ignores two major ingredients necessary for a meaningful relationship: *character* and *integrity*.

While lust and love both begin with the same letter—and often the same feeling—they are vastly different.

While lust and love both begin with the same letter—and often the same feeling—they are vastly different. Lust invariably decreases with time and age, whereas love increases. Premarital sex may be an indicator of lack of character and integrity, rather than love.

6. I [female] want to feel fulfilled as a woman.

The argument often goes something like this: "Isn't it better to test sex with my lover, lest I marry a klutz?" If fulfillment (whatever that means) is all you are seeking, then you have missed the whole point of commitment in a relationship. In my many years of counseling I have yet to counsel a couple who could not fulfill each other's sexual needs. Some needed instruction and practice, but with a lifetime to work on technique, why hurry? Like anything else in life, sex should get better with practice, but if technique becomes the focal point of your relationship, you will probably be disappointed. After all, how many can give an Academy Award-winning performance every day?

   7. *I need to exercise my sexual muscles.*

First, check to make sure you actually know your sexual muscles! The best exercise for sexual muscles is in the mind and is known as self-control. Learning to control your response to sexual urges will make you a better lover when the time is right. One who cannot control urges is an addict, whether it be to sex or to drugs.

   8. *I need to be sure my partner does not have a sexual dysfunction.*

Actually, men or women with true sexual dysfunctions are rare. Even if they weren't, premarital sex is no guarantee that problems will not develop later. In fact, premarital sex may actually be the trigger that causes sexual dysfunction later in life. Sexual performance before marriage is absolutely no indication of sexual performance after marriage.

   9. *I need to feel loved and wanted.*

This person may be substituting sex with partners for love from parents. Sex is not the answer to this person's problems. Counseling and healthy relationships will do far more to meet the needs than premarital sex.

   10. *I am afraid I am gay.*

If you are going to gauge your sexual preference on your first sexual encounter, you may indeed be disappointed. Sex is seldom mind-blowing rapture the first, second, or even third time. This may cause you to doubt your sexual preference even more. Actually, sex with someone of the opposite sex is not a true indicator of heterosexuality, since there are many bisexuals and since many men and women discover or admit that they are gay in later years, long after they are married and have children.

When all is said and done concerning sex, it would be much better if there was a lot more said and a lot less done! One researcher wrote that "sex is only incidental to premarital happiness, and sex before marriage leads more to unhappiness than it does to happiness. In fact, I believe quite honestly it can be said that sex causes much more misery than it produces pleasure" (*Medical Aspects of Human Sexuality*, May 1973).

In his book *No Wonder They Call Him the Savior*, Max Lucado recalls this story that was originally reported in the Miami *Herald*. Lucado writes: "Judith Bucknell was homicide number 106 that year. She was killed on a steamy June 9 evening. Age 38. Weight: 109 pounds. Stabbed seven times. Strangled. She kept a diary. Had she not kept this diary, perhaps the memory of her would have been buried with her body. But the diary exists, a painful epitaph to a lonely life. The correspondent made this comment about her writings: 'In her diaries, Judy created a character and a voice. The character is herself, wistful, struggling, weary; the voice is yearning. Judith Bucknell has failed to connect; age 38, many lovers, much love offered, none returned.'

"Successful as a secretary, but a loser at love. Her diary was replete with entries such as the following: 'Where are the men with the flowers . . . and music? Where are the men who call and ask for a genuine, actual date? Where are the men who would like to share more than my bed, my booze, my food? . . . I would like to have in my life, once before I pass through my life, the kind of sexual relationship that is part of a loving relationship.'

"She never did. Judy was not a prostitute. She was not on drugs or on welfare. She never went to jail. She was not a social outcast. She was respectable. She jogged. She hosted parties. She wore designer clothes and had an apartment that overlooked the bay. And she was very lonely. 'I see people together and I'm so jealous I want to throw up. What about me! What about me!'

"Though she had many lovers (59 in 56 months), she had little love. 'Who is going to love Judy Bucknell?' The diary continues, 'I feel so old. Unloved. Unwanted. Abandoned. Used up. I want to cry and sleep forever.' "

Sex is not the answer to the problems that teenagers face. It only complicates those problems they already have and creates a host of future problems. Teach your teens about sex, but also teach them about responsibility, true love, and how to be a *giver* rather than a *loser/user*.

CHAPTER 7

Teaching Your Teens About Values

A man returned to his shiny new car in a parking lot to find one side badly damaged and a note under the windshield wiper. It read: "I've just smashed into your car. The people who saw the accident are watching me. They think I'm writing down my name and address. They're wrong!"

While I was in the U.S. Air Force I needed to earn some extra money. So my friend Big Jack and I decided to paint houses in our spare time. The first house we did was located in a rather close-knit community, and we knew that a good job and a low price on this house would give us all the work we could handle. We intentionally bid low and did a careful job applying the paint and stain. The owners were so pleased with our work that they told all their friends, and the job requests began flowing in.

However, Big Jack and I decided we had worked too hard on that first house, so we devised a way to do less work for more money on the second one. Since the owners were away at work during the day, it was relatively easy to use the "second coat" scam. Like the first owners, they also wanted two full coats of paint on their house. So Big Jack and I applied a thin first coat on the front of the house, but a very heavy coat on the other three sides. When the owners returned home that evening, we told them we had painted two coats on three sides and had only the front to do. Their visual inspection confirmed what we had said, and we finished the house in half the time.

Recalling this unpleasant part of my past reminds me of a story I heard about Bill and Harry, who started a house-painting business. Like Big Jack and me, Bill and Harry decided to increase profits by using some dishonest tactics. In their case, they thinned the latex paint with water.

Finally Bill couldn't take it any longer, so he told Harry he was through. Harry remonstrated, "Oh, come on, Bill! In a little while we'll be rich enough to retire."

"No way," Bill replied. "I can't do it anymore. Last night an angel visited me in my sleep and said loud and clear, 'Repaint, ye thinner!'"

What does it take to make right decisions? What prompts teenagers to be honest? Parents? Perhaps, unless they see them fake the "second coat" in a business deal. Friends? Perhaps, unless they see them look over someone else's shoulder during an exam. How can teens develop their own set of values? Who, or what, should be their example?

> "The Spirit clearly says that in later times some will abandon the faith and follow deceiving spirits."

"The Spirit clearly says that in later times some will abandon the faith and follow deceiving spirits and things taught by demons. Such teachings come through hypocritical liars, whose consciences have been seared as with a hot iron" (1 Tim. 4:1, 2, NIV).

The story is told about a father who was explaining business ethics to his son. Since the son would someday take over the family business, the father wanted to make certain that he was well versed in ethics. "Suppose a woman comes into the store and orders $100 worth of material. You wrap it and give it to her. She pays you with a $100 bill. As she goes out the door you realize she has given you *two* crisp new $100 bills by mistake. Now, son, here's where the ethics come in. The question you must ask at that point is Should you, or should you not, tell your partner?"

Perhaps the reason we smile is because such behavior has almost become the norm in modern society. Sometimes such behavior is exhibited even by people who claim to be Christians. Perhaps even by parents or friends. It may also be confusing for teens to see someone outside their church displaying ethical values superior to those held by some of their own church members. Assure your teenage children that this is truly disappointing, but because of sin entering into human decisions, it is unfortunately predictable. Even the apostle Paul observed this phenomenon in his day, many hundreds of years ago.

It may be confusing for teens to see someone outside their church displaying ethical values superior to those held by some of their own church members.

"Indeed, when Gentiles [those outside the church], who do not have the law, do by nature things required by the law, they are a law for themselves, even though they do not have the law, since they show that the requirements of the law are written on their hearts, their consciences also bearing witness, and their thoughts now accusing, now even defending them" (Rom. 2:14, 15, NIV).

God originally gave Adam and Eve perfect consciences. They could depend upon their consciences to tell them right from wrong. Their consciences (decision-makers) were trustworthy because God had written His law (values) upon their hearts. They did by nature those things that were both pleasing to God and acceptable in their relationship with each other.

However, once sin entered into their hearts it contaminated the value system that God had installed in them at Creation. This contamination affected every part of their being, including their consciences and their relationships with each other. From that moment on, humans could no longer trust their own value systems or abilities to make decisions. Adam and Eve found that even though a part of them desired to maintain high ethical standards, another part was untrustworthy.

We are all born into this world with messed-up value systems and distorted consciences. It's as if a sin virus has been put into our computer and manifests itself almost at random and when least expected. We can identify with the young man who went to a fortune-teller in order to find out about his future. "You will be poor and very unhappy until you are 37 years old," the fortune-teller warned sadly.

"Well, what about after that?" the young man inquired. "Will I be rich and happy?"

"No," replied the fortune teller, "you'll still be poor, but by then you will be used to it!"

Unfortunately, that is true for many of us. We are so used to consciences tainted by sin that we fail to recognize what has happened to our value systems. When God created human beings, He did not provide a set of written rules to cover every possible situation. He gave people something better: the ability to think and reason, the ability to make Godlike decisions. In other words, God created human beings in His own image. With the ability to create. To think. To determine right and wrong. To act in a responsible manner. To reason from cause to effect. To make decisions based upon the best interest of all God's creation, including fellow human beings.

Unfortunately, sin entered the picture, so God found it necessary to provide a Guidebook—the Bible—to assist us in using our now tainted value systems. This Book was given to help us make right

> **We are all born into this world with messed-up value systems and distorted consciences.**

decisions in an environment contaminated with sin. However, the Guidebook was not enough by itself. So God sent His Son, Jesus, to walk with us and show us that it is possible to rise above our sinful inheritance and establish proper value systems. God also sent His Holy Spirit to dwell within us and offer us assistance in all our decision-making. All of this was necessary because sin had tainted our decision-making processes (consciences) and the value system (law) God had originally written upon our hearts.

The Christian's Guidebook provides four principles that are useful whenever we must make a decision. Encourage your teenagers to think about these four simple questions before making a decision.

The first question that teens should always ask when making a decision is Will it *harm* me?

The first question that teens should always ask when making a decision is Will it *harm* me?

"Do you not know that your body is a temple of the Holy Spirit, who is in you, whom you have received from God? You are not your own; you were bought at a price. Therefore honor God with your body" (1 Cor. 6:19, 20, NIV).

I worked three years restoring a 1957 Chevy convertible. During the process, I took that car apart and put it back together dozens of times. I knew every part of that car intimately because I had painstakingly replaced, repaired, or refinished every nut and bolt that showed the least amount of wear.

When my '57 was restored, I treated it like a Rolls Royce. I always parked it at the far end of a parking lot to avoid door dings. I wiped it down every night after storing it in the garage. I polished it every month. Why? Because I had invested so much of myself in restoring that car.

God has invested much more in restoring you and your teenagers. He knows every part of each of you intimately. He knows your thoughts and desires. He knows your strengths and weaknesses. To restore both you and your children to humanity's original state, God has invested the life of His own Son. He has invested too much in your restoration to willingly allow any of you to return to your former rundown condition. Therefore, He wants you and your children to avoid doing anything that will harm the restoration project He has begun in your lives.

However, it is sometimes difficult to determine those things that will be harmful to us. Our sinful environment creates what is known as "gradual accommodation." To illustrate this point, a tongue-in-cheek story is told about Mother Teresa, who supposedly died and went to heaven. When she arrived at the pearly gates she was greeted by Saint Peter, who was duly impressed by the advance reputation of this famous modern saint. He welcomed her warmly and told her how much he had heard about her amazing ministry throughout the years.

Because of her amazing record of sacrifice and dedication, Saint Peter offered her two more weeks back on earth at any place she would name. She admitted that she had never been to Hawaii and had always wanted to visit there. So Saint Peter arranged for her to have a two-week stay in Hawaii, all expenses paid. There was only one condition—every night she must phone in and let him know how it was going.

> **Our sinful environment creates what is known as "gradual accommodation."**

So Mother Teresa was conveyed back to earth and found herself in Hawaii. After the first day, she put in her required call to heaven. "Hello, Saint Peter, this is Mother Teresa."

"Hello, Mother Teresa. How do you like Hawaii?" he inquired.

"Well, of course I haven't seen much yet," she replied, "but so far it appears to be a most beautiful place and a lovely climate. I'm planning to see more tomorrow."

The next night she called again. "Hi, Saint Peter, this is Mother

Teresa again. Yes, I really love this place. The clouds, the beaches, the swaying palms are all lovely. I'll talk to you tomorrow."

The third night she said, "Hello, Peter, this is Teresa! I really think this place is great! Call you tomorrow. 'Bye!"

By the fourth night the conversation went like this: "Hi, Pete, this is Tess. You gotta love it here! Pete, you don't know what you're missing! Catch you later. Gotta hit the beach. Ta-ta till tomorrow!"

So it is with our accommodation to sin. Teens, who later become adults, become so used to lower values and tainted standards that these things actually become the *new* norm for their decision-making.

The second question teens need to ask themselves is Will it *control* me? Will I become addicted to this activity? Will it control my future decisions?

The second question teens need to ask themselves is Will it *control* me? Will I become addicted to this activity?

" 'Everything is permissible for me'—but not everything is beneficial. 'Everything is permissible for me'—but I will not be mastered by anything" (1 Cor. 6:12, NIV).

There is an old story I heard while in Africa that illustrates this point quite clearly. It explains how to catch a monkey in the jungle. First you take a hollowed-out gourd and put some choice nuts and fruit inside (something the monkey really likes to eat). Then you make a hole in the gourd barely large enough for the monkey to squeeze its hand through. You then tie the gourd to a tree limb and wait. Soon a monkey will notice the gourd with the goodies. Eventually the monkey will reach inside the gourd and fill its fist with food. However, with its fist clenched, the monkey won't be able to pull its hand out of the gourd, because the opening is too small.

Rather than giving up the food and removing its hand, the monkey will hold on tightly. It will jump up and down and go into a screaming rage, but it will not let go of the food. Since the gourd is tied to a tree limb, the trapper can then simply walk up behind the monkey and capture it.

Satan uses the same tactics on us humans. Often we set our minds so firmly on getting the things we want in life that we become oblivious to the pattern of self-destruction that may be present in our actions.

I remember a Christian college student who became addicted to playing Dungeons and Dragons. It all started out as an apparently harmless way to relax with friends. Before long he became so involved with his character that he lost his own identity. He became more and more involved in the game until he was literally living his character 24 hours a day. He would play for days on end, fall into an exhausted stupor, awaken and start again. Finally the obsession became so great that he flunked out of college and found it difficult to hold a job.

How can you know if your teenage children are addicted to certain behaviors? Talk to them about addiction and then ask them to monitor what they do and think about for a week and write it down during that period of time. If they find themselves thinking about a certain activity while doing most other things, they are addicted to that activity. If they find themselves unhappy when not engaging in that activity, that is another indication of addiction.

> **Will this act bring glory to God if others find out about it?**

Question number three is Does it *glorify* God? Will this act bring glory to God if others find out about it?

"So whether you eat or drink or whatever you do, do it all for the glory of God" (1 Cor. 10:31, NIV).

A farmer in New Hampshire took his horse to see the vet because it had a limp. "Doc, one day he limps, the next day he doesn't. What should I do?"

Without hesitation the vet advised, "On the day that he doesn't limp, *sell him!*"

Will such an action bring glory to God?

A young couple took their 3-month-old baby to a concert. As they entered the auditorium, the usher warned them, "If the baby cries, you will have to leave. However, we'll be happy to refund your ticket price."

About halfway through the concert the husband leaned over and asked his wife, "How do you like the concert?"

"It's rotten!"

"I think so too," he agreed. "Pinch the baby!"

Displaying the godly qualities of integrity and fairness with one's friends brings glory to God. Practicing generosity and fairness in recreation brings glory to God. Refusing to look at a classmate's test paper, even when one really knows the answer but just can't think of it, brings glory to God.

Practicing generosity and fairness in recreation brings glory to God. Refusing to look at a classmate's test paper, even when one really knows the answer but just can't think of it, brings glory to God.

A few years ago Charles Colson was on Bill Buckley's television program, talking about restitution and criminal justice. Jack Eckerd (founder of Eckerd Drugs) saw the program and phoned Charles a few days later and asked him to come to Florida to do something about criminal justice in that state. Together with the Florida attorney general and president of the state senate, Colson and Eckerd boarded Eckerd's Lear jet and went around Florida advocating criminal justice reforms.

Everywhere they went Jack Eckerd would introduce Charles Colson to the crowd by saying, "This is Chuck Colson, my friend; I met him on Bill Buckley's television program. He's born again. I'm not. I wish I were." Then he would sit down. Colson would speak and later, back on the jet, he would tell Eckerd about Jesus. At the

Teaching Your Teens About Values

next stop there would be the same introduction, and on the plane Colson would again tell him about Jesus.

When they finally parted, Chuck gave Jack some reading material and later sent Jack some books that he had authored. Eventually Jack read the books, including the story "Watergate and the Resurrection," out of Chuck's book *Loving God*. Through Chuck's witnessing and the power of the written word, Jack Eckerd became convinced that Jesus was indeed Lord and had been resurrected from the dead. He called Chuck to tell him of his new belief and love for Jesus. When he finished speaking, Chuck told him, "You have been born again!"

Jack replied, "No, I haven't—I haven't felt anything."

Chuck assured him that he was indeed born again and had a prayer of dedication with him right there on the phone.

Jack was thrilled! Shortly thereafter he walked into one of his drugstores and saw *Playboy* and *Penthouse* magazines on the shelf. He'd seen them there many times before, and it had never bothered him. But now he saw them through the eyes of Jesus. Jack went back to his office and called his president. "Take *Playboy* and *Penthouse* out of my stores!"

In 1,700 stores across America, because one man wanted to glorify God, *Playboy* and *Penthouse* magazines were removed virtually overnight.

His president protested, "You can't mean that, Mr. Eckerd. We make $3 million a year from those magazines."

Eckerd was adamant. "Take them out of my stores . . . now!"

So in 1,700 stores across America, because one man wanted to glorify God, those magazines were removed virtually overnight. Colson called Jack Eckerd and asked him specifically if he did that because of his commitment to Christ.

"Why else would I give away $3 million?" Jack replied. "The Lord wouldn't let me off the hook."

But the story doesn't end there. Later Jack Eckerd wrote a letter to all the other drugstore operators in the United States and stated, "I have taken them [*Playboy* and *Penthouse*] out of my stores. Why don't you take them out of yours?"

Not a single owner replied! So he wrote them more letters. By this time the news of Eckerd's decision had brought a flood of customers into his stores because he had removed those magazines. It is interesting that the balance sheet often tips the scales in matters such as these. During the next 11 months Peoples Drug, Dart Drug, and Revco Drug each removed the magazines. About the same time, the pornography commission was deliberating in Washington over what recommendations to make to the president and Congress. While the commission debated, Jack Eckerd acted. Despite worries about being sued by the American Civil Liberties Union, Jack Eckerd removed the magazines. Eckerd's decision to glorify God mushroomed until even the 7-11 stores (the chairman of which sits on Jack Eckerd's board) removed them from their 5,000 outlets. In less than a year *Playboy* and *Penthouse* were removed from 11,000 outlets because one man decided to glorify God with his life.

The final question that teenagers should ask concerning any activity is What will it *do* to my thoughts?

The final question that teenagers should ask concerning any activity is What will it *do* to my thoughts? What will go through my mind as a result of this activity? What will be the residual effect from this activity? Will it be uplifting or downgrading?

"Finally, brothers, whatever is true, whatever is noble, whatever is right, whatever is pure, whatever is lovely, whatever is admirable—if anything is excellent or praiseworthy—think about such things" (Phil. 4:8, NIV).

There is always the danger that a bad decision will sear your teenage children's consciences, thus making it even more difficult for them to determine right from wrong. Around 1890 a man drove by the farm of Mrs. John R. McDonald. A sudden gust of wind caught his black derby hat and blew it onto the McDonald property. He looked in vain for the hat and eventually drove off bareheaded. Mrs. McDonald retrieved the hat and for the next 45 years it was worn by various members of her family until it was worn out. She then advertised in the local paper to find the owner of the hat, saying, "It has been on my conscience for 45 years."

That is a long time to suffer with a guilty conscience because of a decision that she knew to be wrong from the very beginning. One has to wonder if this one decision had negative repercussions in other areas of her life.

Teach your adolescent youngsters that it is always dangerous to pursue impure thoughts lest they linger and become the norm in their lives.

> **God is not nearly as concerned with telling us what to do as He is with teaching us how to think.**

I read of a man who sent a check to the Internal Revenue Service. He stated, "I can't sleep; my conscience is bothering me. Enclosed find a check for $150. If I still can't sleep, I will send you the balance."

I am convinced that God is not nearly as concerned with telling us what to do and when we should do it as He is with teaching us how to think and make decisions in a godlike manner.

We are sons and daughters of God. He created us to use our God-given intelligence to make proper decisions. That is why God offers us principles to use in decision-making rather than a 1,000-volume encyclopedia covering every temptation or decision known to humanity. Fortunately, your teenagers don't have to memorize a set of encyclopedias, just these four basic principles.

1. Will it *harm* me?
2. Will it *control* me?
3. Will it *glorify* God?
4. What will it *do* to my thoughts?

Every decision they must make in life can be correctly handled if they put these four principles into action. God has given them consciences (sin-seared though they may be), His Son as an example, His Word as their guidebook, and His Spirit to dwell within them to help them overcome their inherited sinful tendencies. Now it is up to them!

I heard about an elderly man who had lost his arm in an accident a number of years ago. At first the trauma of the loss totally destroyed the man's desire to attend or enter any sports, even though he had previously been a sports enthusiast. This setback sent him into severe depression. However, one day a friend talked him into playing a game of handball. From that moment he was hooked. Amazingly, the depression left him almost instantly.

1. Will it *harm* me?
2. Will it *control* me?
3. Will it *glorify* God?
4. What will it *do* to my thoughts?

Within a few years he was considered one of the best handball players in his area. He had won a number of important tournaments and always made the game look so easy. In one particular tournament he made it all the way into the finals, where he won two games against one of handball's best players, even though the opponent was 30 years younger.

In an interview with the local newspaper the handicapped man was asked, "How did you do it?"

His reply was a single word: "Decisions!"

"What do you mean, decisions?" pressed the reporter.

"It's easy," the man replied. "Every time the ball was hit to my opponent, he had to decide which hand to hit it with. However, when the ball was hit to me, it was easy, because I had already made my decision."

Think about it! Wouldn't it be much easier if every time Satan hit temptation into your teenage children's "court" they had already decided how they were going to return it?

CHAPTER 8

Teaching Your Teens About Love

One of the longest and perhaps simplest love letters ever written was by Marcel de Leclure, a French painter, in 1875. His work of love contained one phrase: "I love you!" written 1,875,000 times. This figure is only a fraction of the actual number of times "I love you" was uttered and written in the course of this unusual letter. Actually, Marcel did not write the letter but hired a scribe to do it for him. However, in keeping with the scribal tradition, Marcel said the phrase out loud . . . the scribe wrote it down . . . and then repeated the phrase back to Marcel. Therefore, Marcel uttered the phrase 1,875,000 times . . . the scribe wrote it down 1,875,000 times . . . and then repeated it back to Marcel 1,875,000 times . . . for a grand total of 5,625,000 times before this unusual love letter was finally dispatched to his loved one.

About 200 years ago a well-known encyclopedia discussed the word "atom" using only four lines, but devoted five full pages to an explanation of love. A recent edition of the same encyclopedia devotes five pages to explaining the word "atom" but has omitted the word "love" entirely.

Little 4-year-old Mary was hugging a dolly in each of her pudgy arms as she looked wistfully up at her mother and complained, "Mama, I love them and love them, but they never love me back!" Mary is already wondering about one of the greatest challenges humans face—giving and receiving love.

What is this thing called love? Why is it such a vital part of life? How is it that everyone seems to be searching for love but so very few actually find it? Most of us want desperately to be loved. When our need to be loved is not met, frustration and insecurity set in. Many know very little about love or even how to find it. It is rarely explained in terms that are easily understood. A few individuals have had the advantage of taking a college class on love. Fewer still have a master's or doctorate in love. Yet everyone is expected to understand love and how to give and receive it.

For ease of understanding I have divided love into three faces: an *if* face, a *because* face, and an *in spite of* face. For teenagers learning about love, it is helpful for them to understand love as a face they wear in the presence of another person. While the wearing of faces may seem rather artificial, it will help teens understand how love determines every relationship. Love's different faces determine how teens relate to their parents and to each other. It determines how they feel about family, friends, school, and even work.

> **Love's different faces determine how teens relate to their parents and to each other. It determines how they feel about family, friends, school, and even work.**

Unfortunately, the most common face of love in our society is also the most self-centered. "I will love you *if* . . ." is a common phrase heard in many relationships. Sometimes the phrase is not actually spoken, but merely implied. Either way the point is quite clear. I will receive love from you *if* I meet your needs, wants, expectations, etc.

The motive for *if* love is always selfish. It is both self-seeking and self-exalting. It reminds me of the story told about a lion that was walking through the jungle one day to reaffirm that he was indeed king of the beasts. On his journey through the jungle he stopped every animal he met and asked, "Who's king of the beasts?" He wanted to make certain everyone knew the exalted position he held in the jungle family.

"Who's king of the beasts?" the lion growled at the warthog.

"Why, you are, Mr. Lion. Everyone knows that!"

The same reply was given by the zebra, the monkeys, and a whole host of other animals until the lion came across an elephant peacefully grazing on some grass at the edge of a clearing. "Who's king of the beasts?" the lion roared at the elephant.

Slowly the elephant looked toward the lion. Nonchalantly the elephant extended his trunk and encircled the lion's waist. Picking the big cat up off the ground, the elephant whirled him around in the air, bounced him on the ground a few times, wrapped him around a tree, and then slam-dunked him into a nearby watering hole.

Sometimes teenagers demand love from another person as though it were a commodity that can be bought and sold. This self-centered attitude usually causes bitterness and rejection rather than the affirmation they are really seeking.

Disheveled and disoriented, the bruised and battered lion made his way out of the water, staggered up to the waiting elephant, and with rather sad-looking, bloodshot eyes lamented, "Look! Just because you don't know the answer is no reason for you to get mean about it."

Sometimes teenage young people approach relationships with

the same arrogant attitude as the lion. They demand love from another person as though it were a commodity that can be bought and sold. This self-centered attitude usually causes bitterness and rejection rather than the affirmation they are really seeking. Is it any wonder that sooner or later they run into a rogue elephant with a toothache?

"I will love you *if* . . ." is the most readily available form of love. It is manipulative love at its best and destructive love at its worst. It usually reveals the true motives of the one offering it. Teens are especially vulnerable to this kind of love.

I remember counseling with an 18-year-old girl while her 2-year-old daughter sat on her lap. This unhappy mother told me how her husband had persuaded her to have sex before they were married by saying, "If you really love me, you will make me happy." By that he meant, "If you really love me, you will have sex with me." She became pregnant and later married him because of family pressure. Even as we spoke, her husband was out with another young woman, offering her the same selfish face of love.

Many marriages break up because they are founded on the *if* face of love.

The young mother poured out to me the bitterness and resentment she felt inside. How she felt cheated out of her teenage years. How unprepared she was to be a mother. How unfair life was to mislead her with love. Her life was miserable. She was another victim of the *if* face of love.

Many marriages break up because they are founded on the *if* face of love. Too often individuals are not truly in love with their partner, but only with themselves. Many young people are caught up in this type of selfish fulfillment and realize too late that they are being used rather than loved. Tragically, many parents offer only the *if* face to their children, so they grow up believing this face is a true model of love. The next generation also becomes a user rather than a giver, and the selfish face of love is transmitted to the third and fourth generations.

A young man committed suicide because he failed his entrance exam for medical school. His depression was fueled by his father's *if* face of love. The son knew how much his father wanted him to be a physician and how his father had worked two jobs to save money for medical school. This dream was a constant source of conversation and obvious expectation. Unfortunately, the young man did not have the necessary intelligence to enter medical school. There were many other occupations he could have successfully entered, but he felt his father would love him only *if* he became a physician. Therefore, when he failed his entrance exam, he put his father's shotgun in his mouth and pulled the trigger. What a tragedy when parents only love *if* . . .

> **Despite its positive strokes, the *because* face of love can create competition and insecurity.**

The *because* face of love, while not ideal, is preferable to the *if* face, because it recognizes some value in the other person. For example, I love you *because* you are sexy (or you have a new convertible, or you are popular, or you make me feel secure, or you write romantic poetry, or you remind me of my father). This face compliments them on those things that it finds attractive. It offers positive strokes to the one being loved.

Despite its positive strokes, the *because* face of love can create competition and insecurity. The one being loved may feel he or she must continually earn such love. If I am loved because of my long, black, wavy hair, what happens when it turns gray and begins to fall out? If I am loved because I drive a new Corvette convertible, what happens if I wreck it and cannot afford another one? If I am loved because I was voted Miss Teenager of my community, what happens when I am no longer Miss Teenager?

If teens feel loved by their parents only *because* of certain qualities they possess or tasks they perform, it will be a bitter-sweet relationship. They will constantly be trying to earn their parents' love. They will feel under pressure to perform. The *because* face of love often creates insecurity and fear. Teens may be fearful that those who love them will discover the real inner person they are trying to conceal. They may be fearful that their masks will be ripped from their faces, leaving them bloody, disfigured, vulnerable, and worst of all . . . unlovable. This fear of future rejection may even prevent them from returning the love of someone they genuinely care about.

It is interesting that the Bible specifically states that love and fear cannot exist in a relationship simultaneously. "There is no fear in love, but perfect love casts out fear. For fear has to do with punishment, and he who fears is not perfected in love" (1 John 4:18, RSV).

> **"There is no fear in love, but perfect love casts out fear. For fear has to do with punishment, and he who fears is not perfected in love."**

I remember reading about a beautiful young woman who was tragically injured in a dry-cleaning accident. She worked in her father's dry cleaners after school and weekends while attending a community college near her home. She was engaged to be married after completing college, was one of the most popular girls in her community, and had won several beauty pageants as well as being selected homecoming queen. One day the highly flammable fluid she was working with in her father's store exploded and burned her face, chest, arms, and hands. The features that had been the pride of her family and fiancé were now disfigured and would be forever scarred.

The girl did not want to look at her disfigured face and would not allow the nurses to take off the bandages except to change them. Her parents could not bring themselves to visit their disfigured daughter in the hospital. A few weeks after the accident her fiancé broke off their engagement. Even though her burns were healing nicely, she died a few weeks later. Apparently she no longer had the will to live *because* she was no longer beautiful.

Even though the *because* face of love can be misused, it is important for all of us to be loved *because* someone finds something lovable about us. Therefore, parents should look for opportunities to tell teens why they love them. There is something very reaffirming in such a message of love. Perhaps parents need to tell their teenage kids how much they appreciate some particular aspect of their temperaments or personalities. Failure to express *because* love when the opportunity presents itself may result in a nagging guilt for the rest of your life.

Parents should look for opportunities to tell teens why they love them. There is something very reaffirming in such a message of love.

Note the regret in this letter from a grief-stricken, guilt-ridden husband: "I am not a writer, but I am taking some space in the newspaper to write something special about Kathy. We weren't so special, you know. I'm just a little insurance man, but when someone makes your life so good, you just hate to let her leave the world without some kind of memorial to let people know she was alive. I want to tell people to look over at their husbands and wives and say to themselves, 'Look what I have here.' People take so much for granted. It's as if they think everyone is going to live forever and they can put off their love and appreciation until they have time.

"Here I am, saying these things about Kathy today, and it seems like I never said them to her when she was alive. She'd have come to me now with kisses. I am sitting home alone at night, and I see her in the hallways. I see the furniture we bought, and I see her sitting beside me on the couch. If I could go back again, I would do everything different. I would let her know how much she meant to me, but I can't do that, and it seems like the only thing I can do is try to make other people know it. Look at your husband. Look at your wife. If you think you have things pretty nice, say it out loud. Don't assume that they are going to be there forever. Someday they are going to walk out the door and never come back again. I didn't think of that until Kathy was dead. It's too late for me, but it's not too late for you" (letter in the Chicago *Tribune*).

How sad that we sometimes do not express *because* love until it pours forth in a fountain of regret! How about you? Do you tell your teens what you really appreciate about them? Unless parents learn how to wear the *because* face of love comfortably, they may never have the opportunity put on the *in spite of* face of love.

Unlike the *if* face, there are no strings attached to the *in spite of* face of love. It expects nothing in return. It gives at every opportunity. Unlike the *because* face, it does not depend upon the lovability of the other person. It is not dependent upon that person's wealth, power, or position. *In spite of* love looks past the faults and imperfections and is able to love the unlovable. It finds beauty in the ugly, worth in the worthless, and value in a disappointment. Every human being needs this type of love. Unfortunately, few receive it, and fewer still know how to give it.

In spite of love looks past the faults and imperfections and is able to love the unlovable. It finds beauty in the ugly, worth in the worthless, and value in a disappointment.

Because of the limited supply, the *in spite of* face of love is in great demand. Preachers write sermons about it. Teachers teach classes about it. Parents expect it from their children. Children desire it from their parents. Many have received just enough *in spite of* love to make them desire more. Look around at your circle of friends, relatives, and family and ask yourself how many you really love *in spite of...* If you are like most of us, you will quickly realize that you love many of them *if* and a few *because*, but there are not many friends, relatives, or family we choose to love *in spite of*. How many of your relatives would you continue to love if they ridiculed or betrayed you? What about your love for your teenage children? Is it *in spite of*, or only *because*? Perhaps in your truly honest moments, you might be horrified to discover that you only wear the *if* face of love in their presence.

The good news of the Bible is that Jesus brought to this earth the *in spite of* face of love in all its fullness. He came to reassure you that God still cares. God did not send His Son to this earth wearing three faces of love. Jesus did not say "I will love you *if* you are a good moral person" or "I will love you *if* you attend church each week" or "I will love you *if* you read your Bible every day." All these things are good to do, but they are not conditions for Jesus' love.

The good news of the Bible is that Jesus brought to this earth the *in spite of* face of love in all its fullness.

Neither did Jesus affirm "I love you *because* you go to church each week" or "I love you *because* you pay a faithful tithe" or "I love you *because* you say your prayers each night." These things are also good to do. However, they are not conditions for Jesus' love. All these things measure *our* love for God, but not God's love for us. God does not confuse us by wearing three faces of love. Scripture refutes the very idea by plainly stating: "But God shows his love for us in that while we were yet sinners Christ died for us" (Rom. 5:8, RSV).

God doesn't wait to love us until we deserve to be loved. God does not love us *if* or even *because*. God loves us *in spite of* how we have messed up our life and this planet. That does not mean God is pleased with our actions. It means that God's love is greater than our actions.

In spite of the risk involved, Jesus gave up heaven to become one of His own created beings . . . for eternity! He put at risk the entire Godhead to save a creation that didn't want to be saved. Jesus loved throughout His life here on earth *in spite of* those who ridiculed Him, spat upon Him, and nailed Him to a cross. He gave to those who had nothing to give in return. He forgave those who were unforgivable. He endured the barbs of His critics for "mixing" with the wrong crowd. He endured the agony of Gethsemane, the humiliation of Pilate's court, and the separation of the cross because of His unconditional love. Even the pain of crucifixion was forgiven when Jesus cried out, "Father, forgive them; for they know not what they do" (Luke 23:34, RSV).

One poet wrote:
> Isn't it odd
> That a being like God,
> Who sees the facade,
> Still loves the clod
> He made out of sod?
> Now isn't it odd?
> —Author Unknown

The tombs of *if* and *because* were not strong enough to hold the One who created *in spite of* love.

Jesus' resurrection graphically demonstrates the power of the *in spite of* face of love. The tombs of *if* and *because* were not strong enough to hold the One who created *in spite of* love. Because Jesus still lives today to make intercession for us, His love also lives, *in spite of* the fact that few understand or experience it in their own lives.

Each one of us must personally receive our daily supply of *in spite of* love before we can give it to others. Like the manna given so freely to the wandering Israelites of the Old Testament, *in spite of* love is offered freely to parents and teens each day. The only "condition" is that both parents and teens alike must go directly to the Source for this precious commodity—*daily*.

Fortunately God has an unlimited supply of *in spite of* love. He never runs out. No one can deplete God's supply. But remember that fallen humanity is incapable of producing perfect love. Perfect love cannot come from imperfect beings. God alone is perfect and complete. God alone loves without an ulterior motive (unless you call the gift of eternal life an ulterior motive). At best a parent's feeble attempts to show love are all tainted with self. Parents love, but they expect love in return. Parents appreciate, but they expect appreciation in return. No matter how pious they may feel, few parents can continue to love without receiving some form of love in return. Jesus came to make the impossible possible. He offers us *in spite of* love with no strings attached, so that after receiving such love, parents can offer it to their teenage children without conditions or strings.

> **Fortunately God has an unlimited supply of *in spite of* love. He never runs out.**

Yet what kind of love do teens really want to receive? Do they want the *if* face, with all its strings and conditions? Do they want the *because* face, with its insecurity and fear? Or would they rather have the *in spite of* face, which is completely accepting and unconditional?

Before you answer this question for your teenage youngsters, I would urge you to carefully examine your motives. Strange as it may be, most people tend to choose the *because* face rather than the *in spite of* face. There is something inherently humiliating about being loved *in spite of* who we are or what we do. Our sinful, selfish nature feels more satisfied when we play a role in our lovability. We want to earn or deserve at least a portion of the love shown to us.

It would be hard to imagine a young man proposing to his girlfriend, "Honey, I want you to know that I want to marry you *in spite of* all your many faults. *In spite of* your crooked teeth . . . bad breath . . . droopy eyelid . . . funny walk . . ." How do you think she would respond to such a proposal? Would you want someone to marry you *in spite of* who you are or *because* of who you are? Teens, like their parents, desire to play at least a small role in their being loved. They want to be loved and deserving at the same time. Such a desire is the root of religious legalism. (Legalists say, "God loves me *because* . . .")

Accepting God's *in spite of* love means admitting that as a parent, I bring nothing to the relationship that isn't tainted with a selfish motive. It means recognizing that God has no reason to love me . . . but He does! It means that any changes in my behavior are the result of God's love for me and not the cause of His love. It means that the effort I put forth to bring my life into harmony with God's principles for living is the result of my love for God, not in order to convince God that I am a lovable person. If I accept God's unconditional love, it also means that I then have the power to share *in spite of* love with my friends, relatives, teens, and other loved ones. It means that I now understand what Jesus meant when He said, "Love one another; even as I have loved you" (John 13:34, RSV). With this command comes power to implement it. His unconditional love for me is so strong that it enables me to love others (including my teenage offspring) *in spite of* their unlovable personality traits.

> **Accepting God's *in spite of* love means admitting that as a parent, I bring nothing to the relationship that isn't tainted with a selfish motive.**

The power of *in spite of* love is as close as our next prayer. "Thank You, Lord, for accepting me and loving me just as I am. I know in my heart that I am not worthy of such unconditional love. I also know there is part of me that wants to earn that love. But I recognize that if I earned it, I would not be filled with Your resurrection power. I accept Your love for me *in spite of* my faults and problems. I am thankful You have accepted me as a member of Your family. Lord, help me to love my teenagers and others in the same way, and as I do, please make me more like Your Son. Amen."

Whether or not I *feel* loved at this point is not important. What is important is a sincere heart that trusts God to be true to His Word. I must be confident that God does love me *in spite of* my mistakes and faults. I can then be confident that His love is sufficient and without end. I am reassured that He loves me too much to let me struggle alone in my difficulties.

What is the bottom line for *in spite of* love? It means I can begin to remodel my life in Christ without the worry and insecurity that someday God is going to "pull the plug" on His restoration project . . . me! It means I no longer have to compete fiercely for love at the expense of my teens' self-esteem. It means I do not have to discredit my teens to feel loved myself. It means I can stop playing games with God and myself in a futile attempt to be loved. God already knows all about me and still loves me! It means I am free to share His *in spite of* love with my teens, family, spouse, and friends.

"We love because he first loved us."

Final proof that I have experienced God's *in spite of* love will be my ability to share His love with my teenage children and others. "We love because he first loved us" (1 John 4:19, RSV). I will find it possible to forgive because I know I have been forgiven. I will find it possible to love because I know I am loved. In fact, the *because* face of love is about the best I can do unless I am filled with God's Holy Spirit.

How can parents share *in spite of* love in all its fullness if they are capable of loving only *because*? They probably can't. At least not in the way we normally think. Let me try to clarify by telling you about a well my folks had in one of their houses. The well supplied fresh, clear water to the pipes, but the pipes were old and rusty inside and tainted the water. What started out as clear, sweet water at the well became tainted with rust by the time it came out of the faucet. Did that mean the water was unfit to drink? Not really! Our family drank freely of that water and received refreshment and life from it. My parents did not say, "Well, I guess we cannot drink any water because it tastes rusty." The water still possessed life-sustaining qualities even though the pipes had altered the taste.

So it is with *in spite of* love as it passes through our sinful selves. It comes in pure and untainted, sweet to the taste. But by the time we share it with our teens and others, some of our selfishness has tainted it. Does that mean it is unfit to share? Of course not! It still provides the life-giving nourishment of love, even though the rust in our lives is recognizable. Even a rusty pipe bringing life-giving water is welcome in a desert. Our family and friends are thirsting for *in spite of* love. Why not ask God to make you an artesian well so that His *in spite of* love can overflow on them?

Our family and friends are thirsting for *in spite of* love.

A surgeon was standing beside the bedside of a young woman in the hospital. Her face was twisted into a grotesque smile because a tumor had recently been removed from her cheek. Even though the surgeon had faithfully followed the curve of her cheek in order to hide the scar, the tumor was too big and the incision too deep to prevent nerve damage. Her face would forever bear the results of the surgeon's scalpel.

Her young husband stood on the other side of the bed, looking down at his once-beautiful wife. Together they seemed to be caught up in another world without words. Finally the young woman broke the silence by turning her gaze toward the surgeon. "Will my mouth always be like this?" she inquired.

Knowing that she was looking into the very depths of his soul, the surgeon replied, "Yes, I'm afraid it will. I cut the nerve in order to remove the tumor."

She nodded silently. A tear made its circuitous way down her disfigured cheek and fell gently on her pillow. The young man continued to look at his wife with love in his eyes. Finally he smiled and said, "You know, I like it. It's kinda cute!"

Later, in retelling this story of *in spite of* love, the surgeon said, "All at once I knew who was really standing on the other side of that bed, and I had to lower my gaze. After all, one should not be too bold when in the presence of Jesus."

As the surgeon sensed the majesty of the moment, the young man bent down to kiss her. From his vantage point the surgeon watched as the young man's lips approached those of his wife. Just at the last second he saw the young man twist his own lips into the shape of his wife's mouth so that he could prove to her that their kiss could still work.

Isn't it great to know that God still loves you *in spite of* your crooked smile? Why not give your teenage children that same assurance today!

Also by Len McMillan
ParentWise

How do Adventist parents raise spiritually strong children in spite of the pressures of today's world? Family life specialist Dr. Len McMillan provides the answers you need in this warm and practical book.

Learn how to avoid common child-rearing mistakes, find greater fulfillment in parenting, control anger and frustration, and instill biblical values in your child. *ParentWise* provides proven techniques to enhance communication, advice on discipline, and suggestions for single parenting.

Paper, 138 pages. US$8.95, Cdn$12.10.

To order, call **1-800-765-6955** or write to ABC Mailing Service, P.O. Box 1119, Hagerstown, MD 21741. Send check or money order. Enclose applicable sales tax and 15 percent (minimum US$2.50) for postage and handling. Prices and availability subject to change without notice. Add GST in Canada.

More Books for Parents

Passing On the Torch
Roger Dudley analyzes young people's religious values and what is involved in helping them identify with the faith of the church. He offers practical help to parents and teachers that will make their work more effective. Hardcover, 192 pages. US$13.95, Cdn$18.85. Paper, 192 pages. US$10.95, Cdn$14.80.

Survival Tips for a Single Parent
Jeannette Johnson shows you how to find time for laughter, love, and sharing. She shares simple down-to-earth ideas for relieving tensions between you and your kids, and shows how children can help meet family challenges. Paper, 32 pages. US$.79, Cdn$1.05.

When Teenagers Cry, Help!
Roger Dudley uses actual case histories to illustrate the problems today's teens face, and suggests ways young people can learn to cope with the pressures of growing up. Paper, 126 pages. US$6.95, Cdn$9.40.

The World of the Adventist Teenager
The Adventist Church has begun a decade-long study to discover why young people either remain in the church or leave it. This book examines the preliminary findings about the young people being studied. A powerful tool for church leaders, parents, and anyone else interested in keeping young people in the church. By Roger Dudley and Janet Kangas. Paper, 141 pages. $11.95, Cdn$16.15.

To order, call **1-800-765-6955** or write to ABC Mailing Service, P.O. Box 1119, Hagerstown, MD 21741. Send check or money order. Enclose applicable sales tax and 15 percent (minimum US$2.50) for postage and handling. Prices and availability subject to change without notice. Add GST in Canada.

Inspirational Reading for Your Teen

Money, Sex, School, and Other Obsessions
The teenage mind ranges into subjects that are too hot to bring up with Mom and Dad. In this devotional, teens reveal their secret questions and problems. Then Maylan Schurch replies with wit, wisdom, and compassion. Your teen will discover that no matter what's on his or her mind, Christianity has an answer. Paper, 128 pages. US$6.95, Cdn$9.40.

Insight's Most Unforgettable Stories
After 20 years of printing memorable stories, *Insight* pulls out its best: 60 Christian masterpieces that move you with their power. Surprise you with their honesty. Bring laughter, tears, and a burst of self-discovery. A great worship resource! Compiled by Chris Blake. Paper, 191 pages. US$9.95, Cdn$13.45.

Steps to Christ, Youth Edition
Steps to Christ is celebrating 100 years, but you would never know it from the fresh young look of this edition. Sprinkled throughout Mrs. White's unchanged writing are story illustrations, thought questions, and suggested activities that will enhance the themes of the book and help you grow closer to Christ. Newsprint, 128 pages. US$.45, Cdn$.60 each.

Will You Still Love Me Tomorrow?
This story by Crystal Earnhardt deals sensitively with teen pregnancy, shows the consequences of wrong choices, and points teens to Christ as the way to prevent and heal broken lives and dreams. Paper, 107 pages. US$7.95, Cdn$10.75.

To order, call **1-800-765-6955** or write to ABC Mailing Service, P.O. Box 1119, Hagerstown, MD 21741. Send check or money order. Enclose applicable sales tax and 15 percent (minimum US$2.50) for postage and handling. Prices and availability subject to change without notice. Add GST in Canada.

Inspirational Reading for Your Teen

The Bucky Stone Series
Bucky didn't get to go to academy, so he's decided to make the best of Hampton Beach High School. Teens will join him for good times and tough times as he tries to live for Christ at his public school. Titles by David Smith include *Making Waves at Hampton Beach High, Showdown at Home Plate, Outcast on the Court, Bucky's Big Break, Bad News in Bangkok, Bucky's Close Shave,* and *Bucky Gets Busted.* Paper. US$4.95, Cdn$6.70 each.

Roommates
Kate Nichol traces her junior year in college, focusing on the good times, tough decisions, and personal challenges facing college people. A heartwarming story about coming to terms with yourself, your friends, and most important, your God. By Trudy J. Morgan. Paper, 128 pages. US$4.99, Cdn$6.75.

Tough Guy
In this story about coping with the pressures of growing up, Trace realizes that the smart kids hang on to God. By Andy Demsky. Paper, 110 pages. US$4.95, Cdn$6.70.

A Summer of My Own
How could Nikki ever tell Allan what she had done to her dad? In this story by Bev Ellen Clarke, Nikki learns about forgiveness. Paper, 142 pages. US$4.95, Cdn$6.70.

Just Don't Make Me Do the Dishes
Stephen becomes increasingly rebellious toward his adopted family until he finds himself in trouble at a boarding academy. There he learns something special about real love. By Sharon R. Todd. Paper, 128 pages. US$4.95, Cdn$6.70.

To order, call **1-800-765-6955** or write to ABC Mailing Service, P.O. Box 1119, Hagerstown, MD 21741. Send check or money order. Enclose applicable sales tax and 15 percent (minimum US$2.50) for postage and handling. Prices and availability subject to change without notice. Add GST in Canada.